Sisters

in the

Workplace

Sisterhood
in the
Workplace

WOMEN
HELPING
WOMEN
TO SUCCEED

JACLYN JHIN

To my extremely supportive husband and kids; and to all my amazing female mentees (you know who you are!)

Table of Contents

Introduction

A female senior executive from a multi-national corporation took the stage at a business-related conference. I was sitting among several professional women. As soon as the female presenter came on the stage, they sized her up.

"Look at that tight dress," one of them said. "You can see her stomach popping out. Why would she wear that?"

"And her hair is a mess," the other woman said. "It is so frizzy."

I heard another ask, "How old do you think she is?"

"She doesn't look like a CEO," said another.

They were certainly not paying attention to what she had to say. I am no saint, and I must admit that I, too, had thoughts along similar lines as the women sitting next to me at that conference. I think a lot of us do. But there I was, at that time an entrepreneur, CEO and Founder of a sportswear company, *nodding my head agreeing with them.*

After the female CEO spoke, a CEO of another company (a man) came to the stage. They didn't say anything about his appearance, i.e., his mismatched suit and tie or how big his stomach was. NOTHING. It was then that it hit me how harsh and critical we can be toward a woman we don't even know. I thought, *Why are we so highly critical of other women? We don't do this to men.* When a man is on stage, we barely notice what he is wearing. Women leaders are judged quickly on many external dimensions, from clothes to hair to makeup . . . maybe even our smile or the sound of our voice.

If I were the woman speaking on that stage, would they have been saying or thinking the same things about me? I suspect that they wouldn't have focused on my credentials, or what it took for me to get there but, rather, whether or not I looked "the part."

Since that incident, I've taken a closer look into this topic by reading a vast amount of books and articles about women in the workplace and talking to many working women. While it is true that there are many movements, organizations, and groups designed to empower women in the workplace, I found that as individual women supporting our fellow colleagues, we tend to fall short. While it may seem natural to assume that most women support other women at work and want each other to succeed, that's not always the case.

Of course, as with all things, there are exceptions to any generalized statement, and women can be amazingly positive toward each other. Just think of your friends, family, churches, volunteer organizations, teachers, fellow mothers . . . you name it. What would we do without them?

But in the workplace? That's another story. Women complain or point out the lack of females in high-powered leadership positions, but then we nitpick the ones who manage to work their way to the top. Rather than support the advances of these successful and accomplished women, studies show that we judge them much more harshly and are critical of many more attributes than we are with men . . . and oftentimes with crude speculation. I've heard women say about a particular senior woman, "I heard that she only made it because she is sleeping with her boss."

In Sheryl Sandberg's book, *Lean In: Women, Work, and the Will to Lead* (Knopf, March 2013), she discusses how "success and likability are positively correlated for men and negatively correlated for women."[1]

---

[1] Sandberg, Sheryl, *Lean In: Women, Work, and the Will to Lead* (Knopf, March 2013)

Sandberg contends, "The higher on the corporate ladder a woman climbs, the less likable she is perceived to be. In the case of a man, the opposite holds true."

And that's only one of the disparities facing women on the rise. Women represent 51 percent of the population, but when you look at the C-Suites and women at the top of senior management, you'll see that the percentage drops significantly, from 51 percent of the population to less than 10 percent. Although women hold almost 52 percent of all professional level jobs in the U.S., they are only 14 percent of executive offices and 4.6 percent of Fortune 500 CEOs.

As of 2017, there were 32 female CEOs on the *Fortune 500* list. This is the highest proportion of female CEOs in the 63-year history of *Fortune 500*. People are so happy about the increase, but are you kidding me? On this list, there are double the number of men named John who are CEOs than the number of total female CEOs.

Research has shown that women tend to be more competitive to get to the top because we know there is such a small number who can make it. Studies show that women are less supportive of other women in conditions where they are both under-represented in the workplace, and feel there are only a few opportunities for advancement. So, instead of helping one another up in order to create more opportunities for each other, we end up competing even more.

Other studies have shown that women in male-dominated firms distance themselves from other women when there appears to be fewer opportunities, because they view their gender as an impediment. They avoid joining forces and sometimes turn on one another. For example, when I wanted to set up a women's network, I remember one woman saying, "I don't need this. I have a lot of guy friends already in the office."

Recently I was working out at my gym, and my personal instructor told me that one of the other women at the gym saw me training with him and said, "Are you training Jaclyn? I heard about her when she was working at Morgan Stanley. I heard that she is really a bitch and difficult person." He was surprised to hear it, and told her he thought that I was really nice. But she insisted. She doesn't even know me, but she was judging me.

If an employee has a bad experience with a female boss, they are quick to announce that they'll never work for another woman. And if you look at many movies where women leaders are depicted—if you are anything like Miranda Priestly played by Meryl Streep in *The Devil Wears Prada* or Katharine Parker played by Sigourney Weaver in *Working Girl*—I wouldn't want to work for a female, either.

I've heard many reasons why there are not more women at the top, things like: it is a boys' club at the top, we don't lean in enough, it's the patriarchy, women have family obligations that make it more difficult to work the long hours it takes to succeed . . . the list goes on and on.

While I agree with many of these factors, I think we are missing the elephant in the room—or should I say, the *pink* elephant?

The pink elephant is that there are women who sabotage the careers of other women. There are women who refuse to support each other. Few women can overcome the ranks of their professions if their female colleagues covertly or overtly hold them back. How will we get more women in senior positions if we women add fuel to the misconceptions and stereotypes?

I think it's through awareness, and awareness can lead to changed behavior. There are people who totally disagree with me, and I'm fine with that, but there are also a whole bunch of women who agree with me. I think it's important to talk about it openly. If we are aware of our or another's negativity toward women (especially when it's criticism that has nothing to do with work performance), and if we catch ourselves or our friends being catty or derisive toward a successful woman, maybe we'll think about it for a minute and ask ourselves, "Why are we saying these things? What good does it do to say these things?"

Madeleine Albright once said, "There is a special place in hell for women who don't help other women." Well, if she's right, I would say that this "special place" must be really crowded.

Over the years, I've asked many senior women if they would talk to a young female professional to give her some guidance, and a lot of them won't do it. They say they're too busy, which is fine. But some women have also told me they had to work hard to get where they are and don't feel like helping another woman.

I asked one woman, who was part of the women's 100 hedge fund group and other women's networks, if she could meet a junior ex-investment banker woman for coffee because she was thinking of doing what the hedge fund person was doing. She answered with, "Do you know how many women want to have coffee with me? I've had to work hard to get to where I am, and they should figure it out themselves." I was surprised and appalled by her response.

Research, as well as anecdotal information, calls it the "Queen Bee" syndrome. The term was coined in the 1970s, following a study led by researchers at the University of Michigan. Even though the study was done in the seventies, there is plenty of new research that finds that one of the major reasons we don't see women being promoted is because women at higher levels do not help other women get ahead.

Women at the top experience something called "value threat," which causes them to not want to help other women. One article analogized it to "rope ladders;" that is, when women climb to senior positions, they promptly haul up the ladder right behind them. They found that women who achieved success in male-dominated environments feel threatened by other women, which makes them more likely to oppose the rise of other women.

Another explanation is what I call the "D.I.Y. Bootstrap Theory," which goes like this: "If I had to pull myself up by the bootstraps to get ahead with no one to help me, why should I help you? Do it yourself!" That is exactly what the hedge fund woman was doing.

Throughout my 20-year legal and finance career, I hoped I could find some great female role models to help me, but I wasn't able to—either because there weren't any, or the ones I knew weren't people I wanted to emulate. In fact, some of the senior women I've met in the workplace have been very mean—they would say nice things to my face, but stab me in the back.

I'm not saying that we're all like this. I'm not merely trying to point out negatives and flaws. I just want us to talk about it. I want to make women aware of our culpability. Some of us are afraid to look and become aware, because we know the fingers we've been pointing at others will be pointing back at us.

There are a lot of books that discuss inequality in the workplace and, many people have different theories as to why it still exists. But the main theme I want to address in this book is a concept I am passionate about, and that is *sisterhood*. I believe we can help close this disparity by bringing sisterhood into the workplace.

For me, sisterhood is about helping one another with genuine love and caring. It's not at a superficial level of just, "I know her, she's an acquaintance," or "She works in this or that department." It goes much deeper.

I grew up with three sisters, and I know the difference between a real sister and an acquaintance in the workplace. For me, sisterhood represents a "real" relationship among women who are proud and supportive of one another's success. Although I know sisters may not always agree with each other and may argue a lot, the underlying assumption is that you are expected to be supportive and try to get along.

In certain industries, especially in those that are male-dominated like technology, finance, and law, I find that sisterhood is lacking to an even higher degree. Oftentimes, I ask myself, *Where is it?*

I've been searching to find out and provide solutions to cultivate sisterhood at work. That's what this book is all about.

What if I said things could get better, and that it starts with you and with me? And it is most assuredly up to us . . . the women. You will find ideas here that will challenge you to let go of the stereotypes about women, and our relationships with each other in the workplace . . . relationships that lead to competitiveness, cattiness, derisiveness, and our unwillingness to look at the real problem.

Some of us blame men in senior positions for not requiring and/or encouraging more women at the top. But maybe we should take a real hard look at ourselves. It is time to take an honest look at how we treat one another in the workplace, and strive for greater professionalism and support for one another.

And we can do that by using the principles of this one word—SISTERHOOD.

Our sisters at work are not people to fear or rally against. In fact, whenever you take an adversarial attitude toward anyone or anything, you give away your power. Instead of being jealous, resentful, or resistant to helping other women find their strengths and positions in the corporate world, you'll be able to invoke the power and pleasure of sisterhood.

We are women, we are amazing, we are doers, and we can change this. We can change it by being sisters at work.

Chapter 1

Our Unique Differences with Men—Is it Our DNA?

Is it possible that the foundation of the problem starts with our biology and our "hard-wiring" to compete with other women?

In a *New York Times* article by Emily V. Gordon titled, "Why women compete with each other,"[1] Gordon writes that there are two main theories of why women are competitive in indirectly aggressive ways. The first is based on evolutionary psychology and the other is feminist psychology.

> "Evolutionary psychology, which uses natural selection to explain our modern behaviors, says that women need to protect themselves (read: their wombs) from physical harm, so indirect aggression keeps us safe while lowering the stock of other women."

There are numerous theories, backed up by decades of research, that say it's in our DNA. As the gender that is smaller and with less muscle mass, we are constantly aware of and monitor for our safety . . . whether consciously or unconsciously. If someone seems threatening,

---

[1] Emily V. Gordon, "Why women compete with each other," (*New York Times*, 2015), http://www.nytimes.com/2015/11/01/opinion/sunday/why-women-compete-with-each-other.html?_r=0

it creates tension, a woman reacts, and then there is relief. If a woman poses a threat, she's kicked out of the tribe. In high school, it's cliques. In the workplace, it's the boardroom. There's only so much room at the top, or so we think. It is all governed by instinct—cavewoman instinct.

Joyce Benenson, a psychologist at Emmanuel College in Boston, believes that women undermine one another because they have always had to compete for mates and for resources for their offspring. "Other female competitors must be kept away. An unrelated woman, kind and reassuring and similar as she may be, nonetheless is a competitor. A mother must weigh the benefit of having a close relationship with an unrelated woman (who has a lot in common with her) against the cost that this other woman might steal her food or run off with her husband."[2]

As for feminist psychology, Noam Shpancer writes in *Psychology Today*:

> . . . competition among females is driven primarily not by biological imperatives but rather by social mechanisms. According to this argument, cutthroat female competition is mainly due to the fact that women, born and raised in a male-dominated society, internalize the male perspective (the "male gaze") and adopt it as their own. The male view of women as primarily sexual objects becomes a self-fulfilling prophecy. As women come to consider being prized by men their ultimate source of strength, worth, achievement and identity, they are compelled to battle other women for the prize.[3]

---

[2] Benenson, Joyce F. and Markovits, Henry, *Warriors and Worriers: The Survival of the Sexes*,

[3] Shpancer, Noam, "Feminine Foes: New Science Explores Female Competition," (*Psychology Today*, 2014), https://www.psychologytoday.com/intl/blog/insight-therapy/201401/feminine-foes-new-science-explores-female-competition

Regardless of which theory could be potentially correct, both suggest that women mainly compete using indirect aggression. Author Kaj Bjorkqvist, Professor of Developmental Psychology at Finland's Abo Akademi University, is known for his extensive research into the topic of aggression. According to Dr. Björkqvist's findings on gender differences in aggression:

Females prefer to use indirect aggression over direct aggression (i.e., verbal and physical aggression) because this form of aggression maximizes the harm inflicted on the victim while minimizing the personal danger involved. The risk to the perpetrator is lower because she often remains anonymous, thereby avoiding a counterattack. As well, indirect aggression harms others in such a socially skilled manner that the aggressor can also make it appear as if there was no intention to hurt at all.[4]

These relatively low-risk competitive strategies are usually favored by women, probably due to constraints of offspring production and care. For females, it is more important that they stay alive so their offspring's chances of survival improve. Therefore, indirect aggression is a low cost (i.e., whereas, direct aggression can result in physical injury and even death), but effective, form of competition among young women.[5]

In fact, according to Benenson, competition between unrelated females is hard to spot because, in the face of things, women go to great lengths to be nice. "Women focus on whether they and their children are surviving and thriving. They must compete to do so, but because

---

[4] https://link.springer.com/article/10.1007percent2FBF01420988

[5] Vaillancourt, Tracy, Do human females use indirect aggression as an intrasexual competition strategy? Royal Society Publishing, December 2013, https://royalsocietypublishing.org/doi/full/10.1098/rstb.2013.0080

women always must be very careful to avoid retaliation, they must do so in private."[6]

What are these types of indirect aggression? Indirect aggression can include things like excluding people from the group, criticizing a competitor's appearance, giving them the silent treatment, or spreading rumors about the person.

In a literature review by Tracy Vaillancourt in 2013,[7] she espoused that women have a particular proclivity for using indirect aggression, which is typically directed at other females. According to her study, females have primarily focused on two competitive strategies to attract men: (i) "self-promotion," making themselves look more physically attractive (wearing make-up or sexy clothing) and (ii) the "derogation of rivals" (being disparaging about another woman's appearance or being catty by spreading negative rumors about other women).[8]

While these theories may show why women may be biologically wired to be more competitive with other women, and use indirect aggression to do so, what does it mean for us now? Does it mean that there is nothing we can do about it? Of course not! In fact, I believe we *can* do something about it—if we are willing to talk about the issues and address them. You can't change what you don't recognize and acknowledge, so the first step to solving any problem is recognizing that there may be a problem.

That's my goal for this book.

Let's bring awareness to the problems that are experienced by women specifically in the workplace—problems that men rarely, if ever, have to consider. Through awareness, we will be better equipped to examine and manifest solutions. If we know that we may be wired to be competitive with each other, then when we feel envious or jealous of another woman, we should notice and acknowledge it. Then, reflect

---

[6] Benenson, *Warriors and Worries,* page 174

[7] Vaillancourt, Ibid. vi

[8] https://www.ncbi.nlm.nih.gov/pmc/articles/PMC3826209/]

on why we think or feel this way and whether it is justified. We should put those feelings aside consciously and make the effort to stop ourselves from taking indirect aggressive actions that cause distance among the sisters, which can result in pervasive problems for women in the workplace. Let's take a closer look at how these indirect aggression, such as disparaging remarks, ends up hurting the sisterhood.

DISPARAGING REMARKS

Social Media Shaming

Trolling has become an established term for people who sow discord on the Internet by starting arguments—and there are a lot of them around. Women seem to be particularly prone—a survey conducted by cosmetics firm Dove and Twitter found that in 2014 over five million negative tweets were posted about beauty and body image—and four out of five of them appeared to come from women.

In an article for thedailybeast.com, titled "Mean Girls" and Beyond: Is Social Media Killing Female Friendships?"[9], Lizzie Crocker writes about a 27-year-old woman and how she feels intentionally excluded and rejected by a group of longtime girlfriends—not in person so much as in their online communications.

They don't "like" her Facebook posts and photos with the same enthusiasm or frequency as they do each other's. Her phone buzzes constantly with their gushing group WhatsApp chats, yet whenever she chimes in, they ignore her contributions.

"It sounds like a high school problem," she writes, "but I pick up bad vibes and feel like they don't like me . . . It seems unhealthy. Especially bad since they are old friends."

---

[9] Crocker, Lizzie, "Mean Girls and Beyond: Is Social Media Killing Female Friendships?" (The Daily Beast, 2017), https://www.thedailybeast.com/mean-girls-and-beyond-is-social-media-killing-female-friendships

Yes, it does sound like a high school problem—like a scene from a *Mean Girls* sequel set in our digital times. But the dynamics of female friend groups and odd-girl-out syndromes don't disappear after high school, and communicating in group texts or through messaging apps has added new layers of complexity to traditional female friendship dynamics. In an article titled, "Why Women Hate Women (on social media),"[10] Rowena Nagy writes:

> A UK study by Scope has found that, of the 1,500 people surveyed, 62 percent felt inadequate and jealous when they compared their achievements and life events to those of their friends on social media. This unjustified jealousy is not a new thing. For a long time, women have compared themselves to, judged and even been jealous of each other, for what seems like every reason under the sun. Why do women hate women? If we are the 'fairer sex,' then why is it that some of us like nothing more than tearing each other down instead of building each other up?

Shoba Rao, the author of "Jealousy, Sex and Mummies: Why Women Hate Women," asserts in her article that jealousy is the main reason women hate each other. Rao writes, "Very few people will pat you on the back and say, 'well done.' There's a million and one women out there hoping you fail. It highlights their own insecurities, they find a reason to hate other women, and they end up projecting their own insecurities."[11] I'm not sure that I completely agree with Rao, because "hate" is a very strong word. But it is something to think about—i.e., are our own insecurities leading us to make disparaging remarks against other women?

---

[10] Nagy, Rowena, "Why Women Hate Women (on Social Media), Business Woman Media, 2014, https://www.thebusinesswomanmedia.com/why-women-hate-women-social-media/

[11] Rao, Sharon, The Advertiser, September 8, 2013 https://www.adelaidenow.com.au/jealousy-sex-and-mummies-why-women-hate-women/news-story/515af16f83df0d4f18b51b8b728d6aea

Attacks On Females Who Are Public Figures

There aren't that many women who are public figures and who set a great example or hold a senior position in government. When we do have such women, we should be applauding them, rather than making disparaging remarks. As an example, look at what happened to Chrissy Teigen who went out to dinner after her baby was born. Seriously, her big crime was eating.[12]

She fired back[13] and got some help from her husband, John Legend. He said, "Funny there's no dad-shaming. When both of us go out to dinner, shame both of us so Chrissy doesn't have to take it all. We'll split it."[14]

Women, even women who are trying to do the right thing, just can't win.

Another example is what happened to Sheryl Sandberg after *Lean In* was published. Sandberg's informative book was written with the intention of helping other working women. Yet, so many women said they disliked her. The backlash was immediate, surprising, and had little to do with the points she was making to help women, but rather more about her wealth and perceived privilege. Like Caroline Cakebreak wrote, "As a wealthy CEO, how can Sandberg understand

[12] Krauser, Emily, Chrissy Teigen Cheekily Responds to Twitter Backlash After Going on First Post-Baby Date Night With John Legend, ETOnline.com, April 2016, http://www.etonline.com/news/187357_chrissy_teigen_first_date_night_john_legend_since_daughters_birth

[13] Dawn, Randee, New mom Chrissy Teigen fires back after being criticized for going out, Today.com, April 2016, http://www.today.com/parents/new-mom-chrissy-teigen-fires-back-after-being-criticized-going-t88111

[14] Lawler, Kelly, John Legend on Chrissy Teigen's parenting critics: 'Funny there's no dad-shaming' USA Today, May 12, 2016, http://www.usatoday.com/story/life/entertainthis/2016/05/12/john-legend-chrissy-teigen-luna-stephens-dad-shaming/84272434/

the fact that most of us still have to get the job done with a fraction of the support and resources she has at her fingertips? For a lot of women today, work is about putting dinner on the table and making sure the bills are paid. It doesn't leave a lot of time to lean in."[15]

In a piece by Ted Rall, he said Sandberg is, "the world's most annoying person" and to "Just. Shut. Up."[16]

Many attributed *Lean In's* backlash to gender politics and sexism. Others wrote that we are just not open to like powerful women as much as powerful men, and that makes Sandberg inherently unlikable. But to writers like Cakebreak, "the main backlash to Sandberg boils down one key thing: money." Apparently, she just had too much of it, so her business advice for women was deemed unviable and unrelatable.

For women in public service leadership positions, not only are their bodies, clothing, and hair subjected to zealous attack, these attacks are now deemed justifiable because they're based on someone's opposition to their political thoughts and beliefs. If a woman has a different opinion than today's "third wave feminists" or if she works for an organization or an administration that someone disagrees with, she is subjected to animus and physical threats.

For the first time in history, the White House Press Secretary required protection by the Secret Service in order to live her life in safety. Sarah Huckabee Sanders is an accomplished political strategist, wife, and mother, and she is only the third woman to have served in the position of White House Press Secretary since its inception in 1929. Regardless, she was ridiculed for her voice, her eyebrows, her weight, her Southern accent, and her clothes, while simultaneously having

---

[15] Cakebread, Caroline, The Real Reason Sheryl Sandberg's Book was Criticized, ChatElaine.com, Apr 26, 2013 https://www.chatelaine.com/living/budgeting/sheryl-sandberg-lean-in-backlash-the-real-reason-behind-the-criticism/

[16] Rall, Ted, Sheryl Sandberg: World's Most Annoying Person, *The Japan Times*, May, 2017, https://www.japantimes.co.jp/opinion/2017/05/02/commentary/world-commentary/sheryl-sandberg-worlds-annoying-person/#.W2kVGVUzbcs

women from the other side of the aisle encouraging that she be publicly harassed and shamed.

When Hillary Clinton was running for president, the CEO of Go Ape Marketing, Cheryl Rios, said in 2015 that despite her own success as a businesswoman, she would never support a female president because, "With the hormones women have, there's no way we should be able to start a war."[17]

Around the same time, a letter was written by a man to the editor of the Williamsport, Pennsylvania *Sun Gazette* who basically challenged Hillary Clinton's fitness to be president on the same grounds. I've heard similar things said about women by other women. For example, there was a situation where there were three female lawyers who weren't getting along, and one was considered to be bitchier than the other two. I overheard one of the two other women say, "That girl must be having her period." I've heard that type of language in numerous other situations, and I find it more surprising and disappointing when women say that about each other. When a man says something like that, we are aghast and think things like, *How dare he?*

Another fact that seems to escape most people's attention is that men's hormonal cycles change 24 hours a day, every day. They impact his mood, energy, and performance. But no one has raised that as a concern to hold a man back from a leadership position—or any position, for that matter.

For a woman to have succeeded to that level is impressive beyond belief. We should be more inclined to stand up on our feet and cheer her on as a sister, but I don't see that for her or most other public women. It's time to stop participating in this social media disparagement of

[17] Mosbergen, Dominique, Female CEO Says Women 'Shouldn't Be President' Because Of 'Different Hormones', 'Biblical Reasoning', Huffington Post, April 2015, https://www.huffingtonpost.com/2015/04/15/ceo-women-shouldnt-be-president-cheryl-rios_n_7067564.html

women, and instead consider using our voices to say that these attacks on women and their accomplishments are *bullshit*. Come on, sisters! Let's give ourselves a break. As women, we shouldn't be supporting vicious attacks on other women in professional positions. If we don't stop participating in it, then how many strong, smart, and capable women will reject the aspiration for leadership roles because they know the demeaning comments they will have to endure as a result? To be honest, given all the backlash on successful women, I was extremely hesitant to write this book. I was concerned that there will be women who disagree with me and write nasty things about me and/or my background. I've had enough scrutiny in my life and didn't want any more of it. But I've heard this from Emma Watson's United Nations 'He for She' speech, and it encouraged me to write this book, which was: "If not now, then when? If not me, then who?"

Ruth Bader Ginsberg is one of my role models. In her book, *My Own Words*,[18] she said that one of the best pieces of advice she received came from her mother-in-law, who said, "It helps sometimes to be a little deaf." In the book, Ruth explains that "when a thoughtless or unkind word is spoken, best tune out. Reacting in anger or annoyance will not advance one's ability to persuade." Both Ruth and Emma had tenacity and determination to say things, even though they knew that others may judge them negatively for their remarks.

But wouldn't it be great if we didn't have to worry about thoughtless or unkind words to begin with? Making disparaging remarks about other sisters will only continue to perpetuate and exacerbate the problem of a lack of women in leadership. I think it would really change the way society views us and the way we view each other in the workplace if, instead of being critical of each other in these instances, we were supportive of each other. If you have nothing positive to say, just say nothing.

---

[18] Ginsberg, Ruth Bader, *My Own Words*

IN OUR DNA—ARE WOMEN TOO EMOTIONAL?

I remember when I was leaving Morgan Stanley to start my own business. They had a farewell party for me, and I was really touched by all the people who showed up. At the end of the party, I had tears in my eyes because I thought about my eight years at Morgan Stanley and how it had been a roller coaster ride with many ups and downs, but I was really going to miss my team. One junior female came over and said, "You shouldn't cry. It makes you look weak." I know she thought she was being helpful, but was it really a problem to tear up because I was going to miss my colleagues? I mean, do we really only want leaders that lack emotion?

I've heard people say that women are too emotional, and therefore can't be good senior managers. Often when women express emotion at work, they're regarded as weak. Whereas, if a man expresses emotion, he is showing passion. How many of us have heard someone say, "Calm down" or "Don't be so emotional"? Recently, a colleague came hastily into my office around 7:00 pm in panic mode, saying there was an urgent email we had to respond to. I immediately looked at the email and asked him why he didn't just reply to it. Why was he waiting for me to respond when he could have done it for me? He replied by saying, "Calm down." I replied, "I am calm; you are the one who came in here in panic mode." I was annoyed that he couldn't see that he was distressed and emotional, and instead thought that I was emotional. If women raise their voice, even a little bit, or seem slightly agitated, why do people assume we are emotional?

"Men who get emotional at work are more likely to get away with it (surprise!) than women," says Kimberly D. Elsbach, a UC Davis professor of management, as published in *The Cut*, she continues:

"For men, being angry and expressing it through shouting is consistent with their roles as men and leaders. But for women, even if they're in the role of leader, and shouting might be consistent with their role, it's inconsistent with the role of being female."

It's sexism at work, plain and simple. And while there shouldn't be a double standard, there still is, and it's eroding slowly. "It's a little disheartening," says Elsbach. "We did this data collection in the last few years, and we found that there were still quite negative perceptions [toward women who cried or shouted]."[19]

Even though people tend to believe women are more emotional than their male counterparts, they also believe men and women actually feel the same emotions in the same amounts. It is the expression of those emotions, not the emotions themselves, that differ between men and women. And research confirms this by showing that men are as emotional as women, but they tend to hide their feelings more. Scientific studies show that men and women have different ways of handling their emotions. Men only reveal their feelings when they are under great pressure, as they usually seek space and solitude.

Despite the widespread belief that women are more emotional, a 1998 study at Vanderbilt University found that this might not be the case. In this study, men and women demonstrated the same levels of emotions, but the women were more likely to express the emotions through facial and other visual cues. Hence, men and women have the same capacity for the range and depth of emotions but men seem to demonstrate greater control over their emotions. Comparatively women are perceived to be more open with their emotions, therefore it is recognized that they are more emotional than logical . . .[20]

---

[19] Heaney, Katie, The Cut, How to Control Your Emotions at Work, June, 2018, https://www.thecut.com/2018/06/how-to-control-your-emotions-at-work.html

[20] Women are Guided by their Emotions, PUAMore.com, https://puamore.com/woman-are-guided-by-emotions/

Since women tend to express their emotions more than men, overall, male executives shared "an ongoing perception that women are more emotional than men," and they largely felt that women "need to be aware of it and remain composed." We also heard from men that unchecked emotion by women makes their ideas less convincing and compromises their credibility, because it focuses attention on style rather than content.[21]

Because females are believed to have less control of their emotions than their male counterparts, there is a tendency to believe they are overly sensitive. Professionally, there is a belief that women are unable to accept feedback and criticism without taking it personally. This feeds the misconception that women are less apt to learn from their mistakes and, therefore, grow and improve with experience. The mere expression of emotions has the capability of reducing confidence in the ability of women to be effective leaders in the workplace. It also supports the contention that females are the "weaker" sex and not strong enough to make tough decisions.

As a result of these beliefs about gender and emotions, they directly harm women leaders' chances of success. But even if you try to change by showing less emotions, it still may not work. As Hillary Clinton once told Humans of New York, "If you want to run for the Senate, or run for the Presidency, most of your role models are going to be men. And what works for them won't work for you. Women are seen through a different lens. It's not bad. It's just a fact."

Clinton also said she wishes she could be as loud and animated as men without getting scrutinized for it:

> I'll go to these events and there will be men speaking before me, and they'll be pounding the message, and screaming about how we need to win the election. And people will love it. And I want to do the same

---

[21] Heath, Kathryn and Flynn, Jill, How Women Can Show Passion at Work Without Seeming "Emotional, Harvard Business Review, Sept. 2015, https://hbr.org/2015/09/how-women-can-show-passion-at-work-without-seeming-emotional

thing. Because I care about this stuff. But I've learned that I can't be quite so passionate in my presentation. I love to wave my arms, but apparently that's a little bit scary to people. And I can't yell too much. It comes across as 'too loud' or 'too shrill' or 'too this' or 'too that.' Which is funny, because I'm always convinced that the people in the front row are loving it.[22]

"Women are judged for being emotional," says Denise Dudley, author of *Work It! Get In, Get Noticed, Get Promoted* (SkillPath Publications, June 2017).[23] "We're considered to be difficult when we get angry, whereas men are perceived as being tough and powerful. I'm going to be labeled as a ball-buster and men are going to be labeled as take charge." She believes this standard was also applied to Serena Williams's outburst directed at an umpire at the final of the US Open. "I'm not saying she should have done what she did, but it's an emotional game," she said. "At the same time, a double standard was applied. Had she been a male, it wouldn't have been the same."

Indeed, the same is true in the workplace, as Dudley found. Research shows that men who get angry at work are perceived as strong and decisive, while women are more likely to be regarded as hysterical and, as such, may show more restraint than their male colleagues. "Both men and women are held to norms of appropriate emotional expression in the workplace, but emotional expressions by women tend to come under greater scrutiny than those by men," according to a 2016 paper, "Constrained by Emotion: Women, Leadership, and Expressing Emotion in the Workplace."[24]

---

[22] Crockett, Emily, Hillary Clinton: "I had to learn as a young woman to control my emotions, Sept, 2016, Vox.com, https://www.vox.com/2016/9/8/12851878/hillary-clinton-control-emotions-sexism-humans-new-york

[23] Dudley, Denise, *Work It!: Get In, Get Noticed, Get Promoted,* SkillPath Publications, June 13, 2017

[24] Smith, Jacqueline S., Brescoll, Victoria L., Thomas, Erin L., Constrained by Emotion: Women, Leadership, and Expressing Emotion in the Workplace, Handbook on Well-Being of Working Women pp 209-224

The truth: A man can say the same thing a woman says, in the same tone and with the same body language that a woman says it, and he'll be admired, while the woman will be labeled a bitch. Leadership consultant Doug Sundheim, in the August 15, 2015, Harvard Business Review online article wrote, ". . . there's a gender bias around showing emotion at work. I've seen that in the same places where men get labeled tough, passionate, or open, women get labeled bitchy, hysterical, or weak."[25] It's time we dropped the double standard. Anger is an appropriate response for women just as it is for men when there is an injustice, when someone is being mistreated or when someone is talking over you or constantly interrupting you. Don't be ashamed of your appropriate anger; own it and use it as needed. The truth is you're not "too emotional" when anger is the appropriate response—you're courageous.

I have noticed that, generally speaking, when women are criticized, it affects our performance. It brings us down to the point that, yes, sometimes we need to go into the restroom and cry to get it out of our systems. Why is that so bad? That's when women need to support each other the most because it's a natural part of our being. I can't think of a situation where a woman can't help another woman through her tears by understanding. Instead, women have joined the chorus of men who say, "Oh, wow, she's so emotional. Look at her, she's crying. She can't be a very good boss if she's so emotional."

In her book, *It's Always Personal* (Random House, 2013),[26] Anne Kreamer shares a survey showing that 9 percent of males cry at work, while 41 percent of females admit that they do. When men cry, it is a trait that makes them more likable. However, women who cry lose credibility. For that reason, there are many who conclude that women

---

[25] Allard Alan, 3 Reasons Women Are NOT Too Emotional, WomenWorking.com, Feb. 2016, https://www.womenworking.com/3-reasons-women-are-not-too-emotional/

[26] Kreamer, Anne, *It's Always Personal*, Random House Trade Paperbacks, January 1, 2013

should be discouraged from crying. To me, this is not a reasonable or viable solution.

When I started my legal career, I drafted something for a senior partner. It was my first year in a law firm in New York City, and I thought I did a good job. I presented it to the partner, but I had unknowingly missed attaching the last page. He threw it at me and said, "This is terrible. This is just poor work, sloppy, no attention to detail. What makes you think that you could be a lawyer?" I was shocked. I'd never had anybody yell at me that way, and I'd always done well at school. I went to the bathroom and cried for a very long time.

I was embarrassed that I cried, and it made me question myself, "Can I even *be* a lawyer? Can I deal with these types of criticisms going forward?" After pulling myself together and getting the tears out of my system, I said to myself, "Okay, well, first of all, don't let one person affect your entire career. Secondly, what you should do in the future is, if you don't know what you're doing, find and ask for help from someone who does." If crying is always considered to be a bad thing to do at work, how many other women will think, "I'm not good enough"?

My view is that an organization needs to teach their senior managers that showing emotion has to be better accepted. An organization's culture is most often established, normalized, and reinforced by its leaders. Leaders are most effective when they show vulnerability and acknowledge their mistakes. If leaders are in charge of creating a culture of inclusivity, their work includes getting more women into higher-level positions. And since showing emotions is a natural part of women's biology, a new attitude about showing emotions must be part of that same effort. The message from the top needs to be that no one will lose credibility or be seen as less competent if they show emotions. Rather, they will be viewed as being authentic, while helping to create an even more inclusive workplace culture.

And at the heart of the "you're too emotional" accusation is the idea that emotions are bad and have no place in business. Yet there is evidence that emotions, empathy in particular, are good for business. Empathy is vital for understanding your customers' pain points and how you can solve them, as well as making us better at general problem-solving and innovation. It's important for understanding staff's development needs and motivating the team.

Allegra Chapman wrote a guest blog on Virgin.com, entitled "Too Emotional: Why We Need Empathy in Business," which discusses empathy. There is no advantage in stifling our emotions, and doing so could, in fact, be so negative that it reduces productivity. The negative effects can even make men reluctant to seek mental health treatment. Given the fact that suicide is the main cause of death of men under the age of 45 in the UK, the unwillingness to display emotions can have a devastating effect on men's ability to cope. In addition, the suppression of emotion can lead to aggressive behavior, which can also affect relationships and productivity in the workplace.[27]

People who have an emotional investment in their job can be perceived to care more—about their job and their coworkers. In that case, it can be beneficial to provide employees with the support to display their emotions in a favorable manner, which could enhance motivation and improve employee engagement. I found that during any turmoil in a company, employees want to see if leaders care about them and the company. If they don't see that, their reaction is to flee as quickly as possible. My company recently went through some material changes in leadership, and it really affected me. I was distraught, stressed, and sad about some of the changes because I care about the company and my team. I spent significant time with my

---

[27] Chapman, Allegra, Too Emotional: Why We Need Empathy in Business, Virgin. com, December, 2018 https://www.virgin.com/entrepreneur/too-emotional-why-we-need-empathy-business

team to discuss these changes, and I opened up to them. I believe that since they could see that I was being genuine, they stayed loyal to the company because they wanted to be there for me and wanted to work together to rebuild.

Some of the qualities of a great leader include communication, honesty, a sense of humor, self-confidence, delegation, commitment, and the ability to inspire others. The type of leaders we want to work for also have passion, compassion, and integrity. However, unemotional is not a characteristic identified by most as needed to be a great leader. A closer look opens another possibility—that a leader who expresses and supports emotion in the workplace might actually be more likely to have some of the very traits that make a great leader.

When you notice a co-worker is upset or openly expressing emotions, pay attention to your first response. Are you shocked? Do you consider it a sign of weakness? Or, even better, do you believe that the expression of emotions can be healthy and that it can foster acceptance and growth among your peers? Isn't it time we accept that fact that the fear of sentimentality at work can actually be stifling some of the qualities that produce great leaders?

EMOTIONAL LABOR AND MOTHERHOOD

What Is Emotional Labor?

I have a colleague whose son is three years old. He didn't like eating and would hold in his bowel movements for days. She stressed about it all day. She took him to numerous doctors for help with his constipation. She would go home from work and spend over two hours to get him to eat anything. Her husband didn't seem to mind. His view was that their son would outgrow this. I could understand her worries because I knew, as a mother myself, I would be worried too if I were in her position. Her son was quite small for his age and underweight. It was physically and emotionally exhausting for her to worry so much about her son's health—this "caring" aspect is just as draining as any physical aspect of being a mother. This is what is known as "emotional labor."

In a *New York Times* article pertaining to this issue, emotional labor was summed up as "[the] duties that are expected of you, but go unnoticed."

Mel Magazine, in a piece aimed at helping men get a clearer picture of what it's really about, described emotional labor this way: "Free, invisible work women do to keep track of the little things in life that, taken together, amount to the big things in life: the glue that holds households, and by extension, proper society, together."[28]

Likely the best explanation was provided by Gemma Hartley in her book *Fed Up: Emotional Labor, Women, and the Way Forward* (HarperOne, 2018), which was based on her *Harper's Bazaar* article that went viral:

> "Emotional labor, as I define it, is emotion management and life management combined. It is the unpaid, invisible work we do to keep those around us comfortable and happy. It envelops many other terms associated with the type of care-based labor I described in my article: emotion work, the mental load, mental burden, domestic management, clerical labor, invisible labor."[29]

It involves everything from tending to the feelings of others to managing family dynamics—it is the effort that goes into noticing that people are not feeling well; asking questions and listening to the answers; anticipating needs; reminding them that they are loved and cared for; remembering birthdays and conceiving of gift ideas;

---

[28] Moore, Tracy, The Stupid Easy Guide to Emotional Labor, MelMagazine.com, 2018, https://melmagazine.com/en-us/story/the-stupid-easy-guide-to-emotional-labor
[29] Beck, Julie, The Concept Creep of Emotional Labor, *The Atlantic*, Nov 2018, https://www.theatlantic.com/family/archive/2018/11/arlie-hochschild-housework-isnt-emotional-labor/576637/

complimenting them and boosting their self-esteem; allowing them to vent and listening patiently; checking in on how they're feeling regularly; visiting them when they are sick or lonely; and detecting changes in their mood.

Social settings also involve subtle forms of emotional labor, such as changing the subject if someone is uncomfortable with the topic (and noticing this in the first place); laughing politely at jokes, even if they aren't particularly funny; and focusing on anyone who hasn't had the floor in a while and asking them questions.

Emotional labor and domestic labor are two distinct things, yet it's not so surprising when they're confused. That's because they overlap in areas traditionally seen as "female responsibilities."

Domestic labor typically entails various household chores: cleaning, vacuuming, doing laundry, preparing meals, washing dishes, etc. Not all of this, however, is strictly physical work. Emotional labor enters in when (for example) showing sensitivity to the needs of children, or older relatives—extra tasks willingly taken on that often go unacknowledged.

Emotional labor assumes the *importance of caring*, and involves actually taking time to care.

How is Emotional Labor "Gendered Work"?

Although anyone is capable of performing emotional labor, in reality this work overwhelmingly falls on women. Often, men don't even realize that it's happening or that it takes women deliberate effort—effort that has become second nature after years of conditioning, that is.

While men can (and do) perform emotional labor, they have the luxury of conceiving of it as optional work that can be left to women.

A United Nations study found that, compared to men, women perform more than twice the amount of unpaid work, which includes numerous concerns in the home. As if by default, these often become women's responsibilities.[30] For many women, when they're busy finishing up at the office, they know their work for that day is still far from over.

Why Is That Gender Division A Problem?

Emotional labor isn't a bad thing in and of itself. In fact, the opposite is true: It's the glue that holds relationships together, whether that's a romantic relationship, a professional one, or one with a friend, a relative, or simply an acquaintance.

However, it becomes a problem when women are shouldering more than their fair share of the load. It's exhausting for women to have to pick up the slack for men who assume that this stuff is "women's work," and it's also demoralizing when emotional labor goes unnoticed and unappreciated, which it so often does.[31]

Emotional labor—it's real, but often invisible, according to writer Maddie Eisenhart. Whether it's grocery shopping, managing kids, or holiday shopping, emotional labor is all the work that often goes unappreciated in a relationship, explains Eisenhart, an executive and blogger at *A Practical Wedding*.

Eisenhart, 32, and her husband, Michael, 35, have been together for 15 years. The San Francisco couple have an 18-month-old son, work full-time jobs, and share most of their domestic responsibilities. But for a long time, recalls Eisenhart, she did most of the emotional labor in their relationship.

---

[30] Wilding, Melody, How Emotional Labor Affects Women's Careers, Forbes.com, June 2018, https://www.forbes.com/sites/melodywilding/2018/06/06/dont-be-the-office-mom-how-emotional-labor-affects-womens-careers/#70650eea1103

[31] Holden, Madeleine, A Guy's Guide to Emotional Labor, Is This Invisible Guy Problem Secretly Ruining Your Relationships? Askmen,com, https://www.askmen.com/dating/dating_advice/a-guy-s-guide-to-emotional-labor.html

"At the very least, I mostly just felt really stressed out and burned out and resentful, because I was doing all of this work, and it was going largely unseen and unappreciated, but it's been a process," she says[32].

We're living in a time where women and men are viewed and treated much more equally than in generations past, but there are still plenty of gender stereotypes and norms that are ingrained in us as a society—and these can have a big impact on how relationships between men and women function. When it comes to doing emotional labor in relationships, women are typically the ones picking up the slack.

MOTHERHOOD

When I Googled "working mothers success at work," I got 678MM hits. Working moms know that balancing work and family responsibilities is one of the most challenging obstacles for women seeking leadership positions. As the most-likely primary caregivers for their children, women often leave the workforce during their peak employment years. People often think that women leaving the workforce is a cop out, but I think we should applaud those women who choose to be full-time moms because it isn't easy.

I took four years off to be a full-time mother to my two sons, and I found it very challenging because no one appreciated or recognized me for being a full-time stay-at-home mom. I would go to dinner parties with my husband, and people would ask me what I did. When I told them that I was a full-time mom, they would say, "That's great," and immediately find a way to move to someone else. I felt undervalued and invisible.

Many of my friends who have done both (stay at home and work) agree that being able to go to the office is easier than being a full-time

[32] Compton, Julie, What is emotional labor? 7 steps to sharing the burden in marriage, NBCNews.com, Nov. 2018, https://www.nbcnews.com/better/pop-culture/how-woman-learned-stop-shouldering-all-emotional-labor-her-marriage-ncna934466

mom because it gives us a break from being a mom and provides us with an opportunity to focus on ourselves and other things. But many of us don't go back to work, because we choose to stay home to take care of the kids.

My mother has four daughters, and she was a full-time mom. She never had a rest period when we were young because she had to cook, clean the house, do the laundry, etc. I have two sisters who decided to be full-time moms, even though they went to top universities.

Many women choose to be a full-time mom to raise their children, but many also realize that it doesn't make sense for them to go back to work unless their salary would be significantly more than the cost of hiring help—babysitters, cleaning people, etc. I have the luxury of living in Hong Kong where having a live-in helper is extremely affordable, but how about those parents who live in the US or UK where help is very expensive?

My other sister has her own practice as a dermatologist in the United States and was a single mother to three children for several years. When she was a single working mom, it was extremely challenging for her to juggle everything. She constantly worried (i.e., the emotional labor) about her children's education and well-being, building her practice, ensuring her patients receive the best service, arranging after-school activities for her kids, and making sure there was food in the refrigerator and the meals were planned.

Not only did she have to worry about all of these things, but she would stress about hiring the right babysitter, tutor, cleaner, etc., and handling all the expenses and managing them was a chore. Every time I saw her, I could see that she was exhausted.

Even if women wanted to work, sometimes they can't because it is either too exhausting to juggle everything (especially if they don't have the support of their husband and/or family), or they can't afford to pay for all the help they would need in order to continue to work.

According to the Bureau of Labor Statistics, American working moms cover around 1½ hours more of household and childcare duties than working dads, while the dads enjoy around one hour more of leisure activities on a daily basis.[33]

Among the problems faced by working mothers, Aptparenting. com lists these as some of the most common challenges:[34]

- Extra Costs: Because both parents or a single mom are working, childcare must be arranged, which consumes a large part of the family income. "In countries such as Australia, families who are dependent on a parenting allowance, can find themselves in a worse position because of a second wage. This is because the allowance amount reduces with higher income brought in by the couple."

- Stress: Researchers everywhere have found that "the stress levels of working mothers is much higher as compared to those women who dedicate all their time to either parenting or working." It's no secret to working mothers that the requirements of both roles and endless multitasking is taxing on the mind and body. "This often leads to the women venting out their frustration and anger on their families, which leads to guilt and even more stress. This problem is even worse for single working moms." According to studies, given a choice, a majority of single working moms would prefer to either be full-time mothers or work from home.

- Division of Housework: While statistics show that men have begun to take on more responsibility for household chores as compared to the men of the 1970s, "women still have to bear

---

[33] Mudaliar, Anjuj, Eight Problems Faced by Working Mothers and Ways to Overcome Them, APTParenting.com, Mar. 2018, https://aptparenting.com/problems-faced-by-working-mothers

[34] Ibid.

the major load of household duties. Working mothers also have to work similar hours to full-time moms, and work more than working fathers, and those working part-time have the longest working hours of all."

- Lack of Time for Personal Interests: It's nearly impossible for working mothers to take time for activities like nights out with friends or going to the gym. "Even if they do find time, they are sometimes too tired, and the only aim in life seems to extract more time to sleep each day. This kind of behavior on a constant basis, leads to depression and irritability."

A lot of the issues mentioned above, especially items 2, 3 and 4, can be mitigated if men shared in the housework and child rearing. Michael Kimmel from his TED Talk, "Why Gender Equality is Good for Everyone—Men Included," says, "When men share housework and childcare, their wives are happier. Duh. Not only that, their wives are healthier. Their wives are less likely to see a therapist, less likely to be diagnosed with depression, less likely to be put on medication, more likely to go to the gym, report higher levels of marital satisfaction. So when men share housework and childcare, their wives are happier and healthier, and men certainly want this as well. When men share housework and childcare, men are healthier. They smoke less, drink less, take recreational drugs less often. And finally, when men share housework and childcare, they have more sex."[35] I love his talk. If you haven't heard it, I highly recommend that you watch it.

But sharing is only part of the solution, the other part is for employers to understand the challenges faced by working moms and be supportive and understanding of their plight. When I was starting out

[35] Kimmel, Michael, "Why Gender Equality is Good for Everyone—Men Included," TED Talk, Sept, 16, 2015, https://www.ted.com/talks/michael_kimmel_why_gender_equality_is_good_for_everyone_men_included/transcript?newComment=

in my career, I was worried if there was a teacher-parent conference or school event to attend, or if I wanted to read a book to my son's class. I often thought, *If I take the time out of work and go, and they find out, are they going to think that I'm not doing my job, because I'm taking time away to do these events at school?*

When my sons were sick, I would say I was sick. I also tried to avoid stating why I was taking time away from work for my sons. For example, when my son's school asked if I would come in to read a book for them, I said, "Okay, I can come, but only during lunch hour," and I'd rush over there and then rush back. I never wanted people to know that I was going for a school event because my concern was, *Oh, women and their children, you know, this is one of the reasons you don't want to hire women—they aren't committed to their jobs.*

Astonishingly though, when a man does it, they brag about it! They're able to say, "Oh, tonight, I'm going to a concert at school," or "Today I'm going to leave for two hours for a teacher-parent conference," and everybody's thinking, "Oh, what a fantastic father." They applaud him. Whereas, if a woman were to make that excuse, people don't applaud. They hold it against us. They often say or think, "Oh, there she goes again, taking time away from work."

Chapter 2

Why are there so few Female Leaders?

I cannot overemphasize how difficult it is to succeed as a woman in a male-dominated organization. There is a myriad of things that people expect of you, including your boss, your colleagues, your staff, your clients, etc. It is a constant juggling act. In order to succeed as a woman, you have to be extraordinary because there are so many obstacles in your way. For example, if you're tough and take charge, you're perceived as pushy, bossy, maybe even a bitch. If you stand aside and let others give direction, you're meek, weak, probably not leadership material. Sometimes you're accused of being all these at once.

As discussed in a 2016 *Washington Post* article, 84 percent of respondents said they've gotten feedback that they were "too aggressive." Yet 53 percent also said they've been told they were "too quiet." A full 44 percent said they've heard both: that they were "too aggressive" *and* "too quiet."[1]

This is hardly the only double-bind that women face in the workplace.

---

[1] Rampell, Catherine, "Be Pretty but Not Too Pretty: Why Women Can't Win in Business and Politics," *The Washington Post,* Jan. 2016, https://www.washingtonpost.com/opinions/no-women-still-cant-win-in-politics-and-business/2016/01/21/5529c28e-c079-11e5-83d4-42e3bceea902_story.html? noredirect=on&utm_term=.e6bc3e150d22

If you're a woman and you show emotion, you're "fragile, dramatic, crazy." But if you're emotionally restrained, you're cold and heartless. If you take a generous maternity leave and carve out time for family responsibilities, you're insufficiently serious about your career. If, post-baby, you're back at the office too soon, you're a poor role model for colleagues yearning for a healthy work-life balance.

If you don't ask for a raise for fear of being disliked, your priorities are misplaced. If you promote yourself and demand that your work be recognized, you're punished for being unlikable and denied opportunities to advance.

If you're not sufficiently well-dressed, you're frumpy. But if you're too dolled up, you're vain and superficial.

A *Fast Company* article by Eric Jaffe[2] found that when women violate the behaviors expected of them, they're often punished. If she's expected to be compassionate and instead acts forcefully, she's more likely to be labeled "brusque" or "uncaring," instead of "decisive." The piece also found that:

- Women who succeed in male domains are disliked.

- Women who promote themselves are less hirable.

- Women who negotiate for higher pay are penalized.

- Women who express anger are given lower status.

Can you now understand the challenges that women have to face every day? It is never enough to do a great job—we have to go beyond that in order to succeed. Not only do we have to face these stereotypes, biases, and expectations, but we also don't have enough support and role models to help us along the way. This is where sisterhood comes in.

---

[2] Moran, Gwen, This is the cost of women's workplace emotional labor, FastCompany.com, Oct. 2018, https://www.fastcompany.com/90241506/women-do-more-emotional-labor-than-men-at-work

LACK OF SUPPORT TO LEAN IN AND STAY IN

I love Sheryl Sandberg and her book, *Lean In* (Alfred A. Knopf, 2013). I've listened to her TED Talk many times. She's an inspiration for so many women, especially working women with children, like myself. Sheryl Sandberg was very fortunate in that she had a sponsor, Larry Summers, who brought her up the chain and helped her get the opportunity that she had. She's blessed in that aspect. She also had a very loving and supportive husband. Women need more of that support at work and at home, and I think there's a lot of women out there who just don't have it, and the vast majority of us don't have sponsors to help us.

A lot of women who've made it to mid-level don't feel supported to continue up the ladder, so they don't have the conviction to go on because there's no one there to say, "Look, you can do it, and I'll help and provide some guidance." They don't hear that enough, so they tend to just give up.

We need more than to just lean in, we need to also *stay* in. The lack of support leads to a lack of confidence and energy, so women are falling out. Some women I've spoken to say, "Well, I don't think I'm ever going to make it. I don't think I'm ever going to make Managing Director," and they feel disheartened. As a result, some of them leave the corporate world altogether, feeling that, "Okay, if I go to a startup, or if I do my own business, then I can have whatever title I want."

Others fall out because they don't want to be a part of the unhealthy competitive atmosphere anymore. They have new commitments. They may have gotten married. They may have children, and they don't want to have to deal with the politics and competition at work. If you have children and must take care of the household, I've seen many women falling out since the burden that goes with having to manage everything at home and, at the same time, having to deal with the acutely female stressors of work can be too much. This is especially true if you are in middle management and you're almost there, because it becomes even more challenging at work the more senior you become. Many women fall out before they get there.

LACK OF WORKPLACE NETWORKING AND SUPPORT

Women are missing critical relationships that are needed to change the course of their careers. Women of color have an even greater challenge. The leadership pipeline is dominated by males. And women's networks are not as fully developed among influencers in their organizations.

When I first joined my current company, I noticed there wasn't a woman's network, so I tried to launch one with the help of certain other women with the company. We called it a gender equality network. It was very difficult, because some women said they didn't need a women's network because they had great relationships with the men at work. Sadly the network fizzled out because there were no concrete targets and there wasn't enough buy-in from senior members of the company. Now we're trying to do it again, but this time with more concrete ways of trying to change things, such as a talent retention program.

By looking at talent retention planning and making sure that there are more women on that list than men, or at least 50/50, the company can try to retain these talented women. We need to encourage the women who are on that list, so they can move up and make it to senior management roles.

If a company is going to have a women's network, it's got to show that the network actually leads to something, whether it's more women in the senior management committee or more women on executive committee. It can't be just women meeting women. Support and involvement from the Human Resources Department is also crucial to the success of these groups because they must monitor the progress.

THE LEADERSHIP DOUBLE-BIND

Women often face a "double-bind" in the workplace. The double-bind is "a situation in which a person must choose between equally unsatisfactory alternatives: a punishing and inescapable dilemma," according to a Catalyst study, "The Double-Bind Dilemma for Women in Leadership: Damned if You Do, Doomed if You Don't."[3]

As Catalyst research confirms, despite the numerous business contributions of women leaders, men are still largely seen as the leaders by default. It's what researchers call the "think-leader-think-male" mindset. As "atypical leaders," women are often perceived as going against the norms of leadership or those of femininity. Caught between impossible choices, those who try to conform to traditional—i.e., masculine—leadership behaviors are damned if they do, doomed if they don't.

When people think of leaders, they tend to think of men and stereotypical masculine traits (e.g., independence, aggression, and competitiveness). Yet women are generally still expected to conform to stereotypically feminine traits (e.g., nurturing, nice, altruistic) in the workplace. This leads to a double-bind in which women who exhibit feminine traits are seen as lacking strong leadership qualities, while women who exhibit masculine traits are seen as unfeminine, mean, and unlikable.[4]

Studies show that when women exhibit stereotypically masculine traits commonly associated with leadership-like assertiveness, they are less liked when compared with men exhibiting the same traits. In a 2008 study published in *Psychological Science*, men received a boost in their perceived status after expressing anger. In contrast, "women

---

[3] The Double-Bind Dilemma for Women in Leadership, (Catalyst, 2018), https://www.catalyst.org/research/infographic-the-double-bind-dilemma-for-women-in-leadership/

[4] Clerkin, Cathleen, etal, Bossy: What's Gender Got to Do with It? Center for Creative Leadership, Apr. 2015, https://www.ccl.org/wp-content/uploads/2015/04/Bossy2.pdf

who expressed anger were consistently accorded lower status and lower wages, and were seen as less competent."[5]

Assertiveness backlash places women in a tenuous position. On the one hand, to emerge as a leader, women must adopt traits consistent with leadership stereotypes, i.e., act more stereotypically masculine. But, when women do act more assertively, they breach feminine stereotypes and suffer a likability penalty that, in turn, limits their professional success. Not only do women need to work harder to be assessed at the same level of competence as men, they also need to work differently—treading a fine line between masculinity and femininity. Asking for a promotion, offering unsolicited opinions, challenging the status quo, negotiating for a raise, or speaking up about concerns may help a male employee get ahead, but a female employee could easily end up labelled as "bossy" or worse for the exact same behavior.

Studies illustrate how gendered expectations regarding assertiveness influence performance appraisals. Managers (whether male or female) are significantly more likely to critique female employees for coming on too strong, whereas the same traits are perceived positively in men.

- Women receive "negative personality criticism," such as being called bossy or told to "watch their tone" in around 75 percent of performance reviews. Men, on the other hand, rarely do.

- Women receive 2.5 times the amount of feedback men do about aggressive communication styles, with phrases such as "your speaking style is off-putting."

- Women are described as being "abrasive" far more often than men.[6]

---

[5] Association for Psychological Science, Leading While Female, Prepare for Backlash, https://www.psychologicalscience.org/news/minds-business/leading-while-female-prepare-to-counter-the-backlash.html

[6] Gender Bias at Work – The Assertiveness Double-Bind, Culture Plus Consulting, Mar. 2018, https://cultureplusconsulting.com/2018/03/10/gender-bias-work-assertiveness-double-bind/

However, men don't have this double-bind issue. Allison Gabriel's study found that when men acted assertive and warm—in general, not considered the norm for male behavior—they reported lower incivility from their male counterparts.[7] This suggests men actually get a social credit for partially deviating from their gender stereotypes, a benefit that women are not afforded.

What can we *do* about the double-bind? An unconscious mind-set is like the blind spot in your car. If you know about it, you can manage it and avoid danger. Being aware of this dilemma can enable you to monitor your automatic mental reactions and alter them. If your knee-jerk response to a confident woman is "What a tough woman," stop. Would you think the same thing about the identical behavior in a man? Or is there a double standard? You can consciously choose to widen the range of acceptable behavior for women.

What can women trapped in the double-bind do? Women could protest about the double-bind. Indeed, it is not "fair." It is, however, a reality—today. A productive approach may be to practice shifting consciously between masculine and feminine styles. It is the ability to shift back and forth between the two and trying to have a more "neutral" style. According to a Stanford study,[8] women who can do this get more promotions than either women or men who cannot. As you move up the corporate ladder, you may find more freedom from the double-bind.[9]

---

[7] Incivility at Work: Is 'Queen Bee Syndrome' Getting Worse?, University of Arizona UA News, https://uanews.arizona.edu/story/incivility-work-queen-bee-syndrome-getting-worse

[8] Rigoglioso, Marguerite, Researchers: How Women can Succeed in the Workplace, Stanford Business, March 1, 2011, https://www.gsb.stanford.edu/insights/researchers-how-women-can-succeed-workplace

[9] Turner, Caroline, Obstacles for Women in Business: The Double Bind, Huffpost.com, Dec. 2017, https://www.huffingtonpost.com/caroline-turner/obstacles-for-women-in-bu_b_5432624.html

As a result, if your behavior is perceived to be too masculine, you are viewed as unfeminine. And if you act more feminine, they think you're ineffective or too passive. The double-bind creates a balancing act. You have to stall somewhere in the middle. And I know it's very taxing to constantly be on guard like that, but it is possible. I know that the need to navigate this conundrum is extremely difficult, challenging, and exhausting; however, if we have other women who have our backs when we need them, this juggling act becomes much more manageable. If we have female mentors who can share their experiences on how they've managed to do this, then it also encourages women to lean in and stay in.

LACK OF VISIBILITY

As a professional woman, being good at what you do simply isn't good enough these days. Intense competition in the workplace means you'll need to understand how important it is to be visible, as well as gather a host of tools and skills to ensure that you're seen by the right people. There is proof that professional advancement requires visibility, but said visibility can be quite difficult for some women to attain.

I've heard many women say, "I just need to do a great job, and then I will get noticed," but they get passed over for promotion. Usually, this is because the people who decide whether or not she will get that promotion don't know who she is. In most investment banks, in order to make Managing Director, there is a global round table discussion with all the senior people within the company. If you have many people who can speak well of you on your behalf, you will always have a better chance in making it. So, while doing a great job is a given, being visible to the right people is crucial for that promotion.

In addition to being visible for the right skills and the right projects, employees also need to be visible to the right people if they want to advance into senior leadership. In one company where they analyzed a sample of performance evaluations, women were half as likely to be talked about in terms of being known to leaders and twice as likely to be told they needed to increase their visibility to leadership.[10] One senior woman who *was* highly visible called these connections the "secret sauce of promotions" and said that these connections are built over informal networks.

Think about the drinks after work—you may not want to go, but it is during these informal "meetings" that a lot of decision making takes place. This type of after-hours social networking can become an expectation for some women (even though they are never invited). One woman stated that she received written feedback from a superior, stating that she needs to network with leaders more. Translated, this means that she was expected to have drinks with specific individuals.

If you aren't getting noticed by key people, it's likely that interesting assignments and opportunities to improve your skills won't come your way, regardless of your performance or how hard you work. This gives truth to the adage, it's not *what* you know, it's *who* you know. Get to know them by speaking up in meetings, building a relationship with your supervisors, volunteering to be a team leader, and asking for projects that will provide higher visibility.[11]

One of the challenges in networking is many women dislike going out for drinks after work with the gang because they are worried about what people may say about them. The fairly common reaction by colleagues when a woman and man become close is for colleagues to start whispering things like, "Okay, what's going on there? Are they having a relationship?"

---

[10] Correll, Shelley and Mackenzie, Lorie, To Succeed in Tech, Women Need More Visibility, Harvard Business Review, Sept, 2016, https://hbr.org/2016/09/to-succeed-in-tech-women-need-more-visibility

[11] MindTools Team, Increasing Your Visibility, Mind Tools, https://www.mindtools.com/pages/article/increasing-visibility.htm

One of my male bosses, who was hardly ever in town, suggested that we grab a bite to eat and discuss work while eating. I thought nothing of it, and neither did he. We got a lot accomplished during the dinner, but the next day, when people found out, they were all asking, "Was it just the two of you?" They were surprised, and wondered if anything was going on between us. I found it very annoying because I knew that this male boss went out to dinner with many different male colleagues, and no one thought anything of that. But when he took me out, people started talking.

Another senior man once told me that he would like to sponsor a female but was worried that people may mistake his motives and think he had an interest in her. If people continue to act this way, it will not be easy for senior men to ask a female colleague for a drink. According to a study by the Center for Talent Innovation, two-thirds of men in senior positions pulled back from one-on-one contact with junior female employees for fear they might be suspected of having an affair.[12]

So how are we going to promote more women to senior leadership if women struggle to be visible and men pull back out of fear? We need to stop these "rumors" and "innuendos." While office rumors can be started by both men and women, wouldn't it be great if women were the ones who nipped it in the bud by saying, "No, there is nothing going on there," or "Stop saying such nonsense."

BIAS

Men may naturally prefer to hang out with other men. They have a bias towards each other. In Joyce Benenson's book, *Warriors and Worriers*, segregation by sex starts very early in life. This sex segregation is much stronger for boys. Benenson writes:

---

[12] The Sponsor Effect: Breaking Through the Glass Ceiling, (Center for Table Innovation), http://www.talentinnovation.org/publication.cfm?publication=1160

Boys really want to play with other boys; girls like to play with both girls and boys. This may be the reason that male groups are formed more than female groups because male peers are so drawn to one another, and away from everyone else. This could be one of the reasons that boys enjoy team sports more than women, and later in adulthood, businesses contain many males who cooperate to make the business successful, but while increasingly women are accepted into business, they do not interact with one another as easily as males do. Not only that, but males have set up their group businesses in ways that are comfortable for them, so when it comes time for socializing with the group, women often feel out of place.[13]

Another type of bias is the "similarity bias," which is the tendency for people to want to help and mentor people who remind them of themselves when they were coming up in the company.[14] Since the majority of managers are still men, it's not uncommon for them to see themselves in a male report who may have the same personality and interests as they did when they began working. Even if unconscious, this can lead managers to favor certain reports with extra mentoring and, thereby, opportunities for development . . . thus an opportunity often missed for women.

In a *Business Insider* article, titled "Our Unconscious Bias is Keeping Women from Senior Roles," Melissa Wheeler and Victor Sojo state:

> Affinity or similarity bias is where people seek out those who share their backgrounds, group membership, or experiences. If hiring managers and boards of directors are made up of mostly men who unconsciously engage in such bias, it stands to reason that more men than women will continue to be hired and promoted - particularly men who share the

---

[13] Benenson, Joyce, *Warriors and Worriers: The Survival of the Sexes,* Oxford University Press, January, 2014, pages 66 and 108

[14] Performance Reviews: How to Remove The Top 4 Biases Found In Performance Appraisals, Impraise Blog, https://blog.impraise.com/360-feedback/4-factors-hurting-your-performance-appraisals-performance-review

same background with current managers. This only serves to perpetuate the cycle of men outnumbering women in leadership positions.[15]

In one place I worked, I had a male boss who was married. His wife worked, but she didn't make much money. This boss was the real breadwinner in his family. He would give men who also had stay-at-home wives, or wives who he knew made much less than their husbands, more money for bonuses than married female employees who performed at the same level with the same quality of work. When I asked him why he did that, he said, "The guys are the primary breadwinner and have a household to take care of. She, on the other hand, is married to someone who makes good money, so they have double income." I thought that was pretty shocking. Sometimes I wonder if this is one of the reasons there's an inequality in the salary or pay gap at the top. Since bonuses are discretionary, and if you have men on the top doling out those bonuses, and men are going to support other people *who are like them*, is that one of the reasons for this disparity? It sure seems like a possibility.

RECRUITMENT

We need to make hiring a fair practice. Given the similarity bias, we need to ensure that an equal number of women are interviewed as men for a particular role, especially a senior role. In addition, people who do the interviewing should comprise a mix of men and women, including someone who is from outside that particular department, such as Human Resources. I've noticed that if a man moves to another company, he will want to bring a few of his ex-colleagues with him, and he will be vocal about it. Most of the people he wants to bring along are not only his ex-colleagues, but also his "buddies," which means they will be men.

---

[15] Women in Senior Roles: Workplace Equality, (*Business Insider*, 2017), https://www.businessinsider.com/women-in-senior-roles-workplace-equality-2017-3

The only time I have seen a senior man ask to bring a woman colleague with him was when he wanted to bring his assistant along. Given that the senior positions are mostly held by men, it means that when a senior male moves to another company, it can benefit not only him, but also his male buddies, basically bringing the "boys club" with them. This is why it is imperative that companies ensure that they aren't just interviewing "buddies" for such roles, but rather, all such roles are open to a diverse group of candidates.

We also need to be mindful of any social stereotyping and ensure that we are hiring candidates on merit. When managers are hiring, I have found that if a woman comes across confident in the interview, it doesn't necessarily mean that she'll be hired or that her confidence will be seen as an asset. Whereas, if a man comes across as confident, it's more likely that he's going to be hired. It goes back to that stereotype where if a woman comes across as "too" confident, it turns a lot of people off because that's not how they envision a woman should be. So those types of underlying social stereotypes lead to these biases, even in recruiting.

The McKinsey report entitled Women in the Workplace 2018[16] sheds light on these issues, stating that less than one of every three companies has established diversity goals for hiring and/or promotions. Less than 25 percent utilize any tools that are intended to curb bias in resume reviews. In external hiring practices, less than 50 percent require diversity among potential candidates, with only 25 percent setting that requirement when promoting from within.

In addition, there is a lack of required training related to recognizing and reducing bias when hiring and promoting. The same is true for performance reviews, with only four percent of companies requiring training for those who conduct them and just thirty percent even

---

[16] McKinsey & Co., Women in the Workplace 2018, https://womenintheworkplace. com/Women_in_the_Workplace_2018.pdf

addressing the need to avoid potential bias, whether it is conscious or unconscious.

Not only is there a lack of training or even acknowledgement that bias and diversity are critical issues when hiring or promoting employees, but companies also fail to routinely track the outcomes. Diversity is more likely to be tracked than internal promotions, and there is rarely any tracking mechanism for performance reviews, which could reveal unconscious bias, such as stating that women are more often criticized for talking than men. This is unfortunate, especially because performance reviews are often influential when choosing candidates for promotion.

In addition to the above, there are also concerns when women end up hiring more women. When I moved to a new company, I started to recruit more lawyers into the team. It just happened to be that there were more women who applied for these positions because there are more female lawyers who want to move in-house (for various reasons, but primarily because they didn't want to have to travel like they are required to do in private practice, and they didn't want to have the pressure to bring in new clients). As a result, I ended up hiring more women than men.

A senior male colleague told me that people were saying that I was giving preference to women over men, and that I was biased against men. I couldn't believe it! I had to explain to him that there will always be more female lawyers than male lawyers who want to move in-house. Of course, I would love to have a diverse team of 50/50, but my job is to hire the best, and the best just happened to be women. But I was being penalized because they thought I was favoring women.

In a white paper by the Center for Creative Leadership, they found that male leaders' competency and performance ratings were not affected whether they advocated diversity or not. However, advocating diversity significantly affected how others perceive female leaders' competency and performance; female leaders received much lower ratings for both competency and performance when they decided to hire the female candidate, even though the decision making also considered candidates' capability.[17] The study provides strong evidence that when women leaders value diversity and promote other women, they get penalized. This is because, in a male-dominated environment, advocating diversity highlighted women's demographic characteristics and activated the negative stereotype that they are incompetent and nepotistic.

PROMOTIONS AND RAISES

Women get promoted on performance, and men get promoted on potential. Research shows that women must prove they are capable of succeeding in a role before they are promoted into it, whereas men may be promoted on their perceived potential. That means men often move up faster in organizations. "When a man walks in the door, he gets the benefit of male stereotypes," says Caryl Rivers, co-author of *The New Soft War on Women* (TarcherPerigee, 2013[18]).

Across all organizational levels, a study by LeanIn.org and McKinsey & Company titled "Women in the Workplace, 2017" found that women are a whopping 15 percent less likely than men to get promoted.[19] The researchers say that, at this rate, it will take more than a century to achieve gender parity in the C-suite. In an article for BusinessInsider.com, Shana Lebowitz writes, "Though women and men say they want to be promoted in about equal numbers (75 percent and 78 percent respectively), women are significantly less likely to make it to the next tier in their organization."[20]

---

[17] Zhao, Sophia, Foo, Maw-Der, Queen Bee Syndrome The real reason women do not promote women, Center for Creative Leadership, Sept. 2016, https://www.ccl.org/wp-content/uploads/2016/09/Queen-Bee-Syndrome.pdf

[18] Rivers, Caryl, *The New Soft War on Women*, TarcherPerigee, 2013.

[19] https://womenintheworkplace.com/

[20] Lebowitz, Shana, Business Insider, Oct. 2015, https://www.businessinsider.com/women-are-less-likely-to-get-promoted-2015-10

If it is true that when a woman asks for a promotion, demonstrating her confidence, as well as merit for the job, she's less likely to get it than a man, then maybe the better approach is that we don't ask for it, but speak on our sister's behalf. In Sheryl Sandberg's *Lean In*, she tells the story of four female executives at Merrill Lynch who began lunching together once a month to talk about their accomplishments and challenges. Since they couldn't get away with bragging in the same way male executives could, they would leave each meeting and brag about each others' accomplishments. It was easier and more accepted to brag for their colleagues than for themselves. Their careers flourished, and each rose up the ranks.[21]

When the Merrill Lynch female colleagues did that, it did help them. That's a simple step we can take to help each other receive promotions. If you see a woman who's doing a great job, vocally express it in front of everybody. Say, "Wow, that was an excellent job or a good point, or glad you came up with that." I do that much more after reading that study. If I'm in a group setting and a woman says something helpful or valuable, I'll say, "That was a really good point." It gives her the confidence to offer even more when a colleague points out that she deserves to be recognized. That also alerts the men and women in the room to her accomplishment and a woman supporting a woman, so she doesn't have to do it all herself and be overlooked as being too confident or vocal.

In addition to the promotions, asking for a raise is also an issue for most women. Women are less likely to ask for raises than men. I remember once we had two applicants, one female and one male, at the same level. The man was several years younger than the woman,

---

[21] McGregor, A cheat sheet for Sheryl Sandberg's 'Lean In', *The Washington Post*, Mar. 2013 https://www.washingtonpost.com/national/on-leadership/a-cheat-sheet-for-sheryl-sandbergs-lean-in/2013/03/07/ae8836ba-874e-11e2-98a3-b3db6b9ac586_story.html?utm_term=.c1611b9e743f

but he had the same title as her because he moved firms more often than she did, and with each move he got a promotion and raise. She was definitely underpaid for her level, because she stayed with the same company for a very long time and clearly hadn't asked for a raise. He was asking for another large pay hike in order to join us!

But she, on the other hand, was fine with a small incremental raise from her existing salary (even though she must have been almost 25 percent below market). When I suggested to my male boss that we should increase her paid to make it market rate, he said, "Why should we do that when she hasn't asked for it?" I then told him that at least we should not offer to pay him more, because he is already overpaid. He replied, "He must be good if he thinks he's worth that much." I had to argue with him for a while to finally increase her salary by even a little bit. She would have received more if she had insisted on a larger pay increase. But why didn't she?

In an article for Bustle.com, JR Thorpe asked, "Why is it so hard for women to ask for a raise?"[22] He writes that the problem, as Linda Babcock of Carnegie Mellon University explained to NPR, is that there is a "snowball effect." Women are less likely to ask for raises because of perceptions of "aggression," which are, incidentally, often held by both men and women when they watch women being assertive. Instead, they typically wait to be offered raises, so they're slower to achieve advancement, slower to achieve higher pay, and therefore frequently lag behind male peers in terms of advancement. This is all in addition to the fact that women are often paid less than male peers for the same exact job in the first place, according to aau.org.[23]

---

[22] Thorpe, JR, Why is it so Hard for Women to Ask for a Raise, Bustle.com, Apr. 2017, https://www.bustle.com/p/why-is-it-so-hard-for-women-to-ask-for-a-raise-43454

[23] The Simple Truth About the Gender Pay Group, AAU.org, https://www.aauw.org/research/the-simple-truth-about-the-gender-pay-gap/

Lack Of Appreciation And Monetization For "Soft Skills" Or "Feminine Leadership"

There is increasing evidence and research showing that soft skills, such as connection, coaching, collaboration and motivation, are what's needed in the workplace to be a successful leader. Typically, female leaders use five of the nine leadership behaviors more often than their male counterparts: people development, expressing expectations and rewarding success, role-modeling, inspiration, and participative decision-making. Women, through their leadership behaviors, help to improve companies' organizational performance by reinforcing five of the dimensions (vision, motivation, accountability, leadership, work environment, and values), and particularly the last three. In fact, the leadership styles more frequently used by women are also considered to be the most effective in addressing the global challenges of the future.[24]

Women want to see other people succeed. I always tell people that the best leaders are not leaders who think about themselves. The best ones think about the team. Our job, as senior leaders, is to elevate the team and to help them reach their full potential. The McKenzie study and numerous others show that women are better leaders because that's what we do. We are the ones who care more about the team and how they develop.

Throughout my career, I haven't seen men go out of their way to think about *how can we develop that person*. For example, one of the men on my team had never managed a team before. Two male colleagues said we should get rid of him because he's not good enough. I was the one who said, "No, you haven't given him a chance. Why

---

[24] McKinsey & Company, Women Matter: Time to Accelerate, Ten Years of Insight into Gender Diversity, October, 2017, https://www.mckinsey.com/~/media/mckinsey/featured%20insights/women%20matter/women%20matter%20ten%20years%20of%20insights%20on%20the%20importance%20of%20gender%20diversity/women-matter-time-to-accelerate-ten-years-of-insights-into-gender-diversity.ashx

don't we get him an executive coach?" So, we did for four months, and he vastly improved. Women think like that. We think, *Hey, give that person an opportunity,* or *How do we develop that person?* That's an example of where emotional quotient (EQ) has become a more valuable skill in the workplace than intelligence quotient (IQ), and that's what makes us better leaders.

Men tend to be more focused on the numbers and the bottom line. They are more transactional than relational. But if you inspire and motivate the team, those numbers will get better. If people are not inspired and don't believe in the direction of senior managers, they are less likely to stay engaged. When you engage people and show that you do care, you inspire them, and you provide opportunities, and then the numbers, revenue, and the bottom line will improve. Again, that's not necessarily the way a lot of men who I've dealt with think. They don't have time for what they call the "soft skills."

I find that very few leaders (who are mostly men) are inspirational leaders. It's partly because they're not wired that way. A lot of them have made it to leadership positions because they've generated the most revenue. If we start to think that maybe that's not what we need in a CEO, but, instead, we should look for someone who's the best manager, an inspirational leader, maybe things will change.

LACK OF CONFIDENCE

As we will discuss in greater detail in Chapter 9, confidence is what women need most to overcome many of their workplace challenges. In *Lean In,* Sheryl Sandberg writes that we hold ourselves back by lacking self-confidence, by not raising our hands, and by pulling back when we should be leaning in. Research backs that up.

I know many women who tell themselves, *I won't be promoted even if I applied for that job,* or *I'm not ready for that role.* A recent KPMG study on Women's Leadership interviewed over 3,000 US women and found that 67 percent said they need more support in building confidence to feel like they can lead; and 6 in 10 women indicated that they sometimes find it hard to see themselves as a leader. Nine out of 10 women said they do not feel confident asking for sponsors, with large numbers also lacking confidence seeking mentors (79 percent), asking for access to senior leadership (76 percent), and, as discussed, requesting a promotion (65 percent).[25]

In *The Confidence Code: The Science and Art of Self-Assurance – What Women Should Know*, authors Katty Kay and Claire Shipman write, "Underqualified and underprepared men don't think twice about leaning in. Overqualified and overprepared, too many women still hold back. And the confidence gap is an additional lens through which to consider why it is women don't lean in."[26]

LACK OF ROLE MODELS

Just look at the numbers. In most events that I attend with senior management or executive committee, the first thing I can't help but do is look around and count the number of women who are at the conference. I think it's a knee jerk reaction, because my immediate desire is to find camaraderie with other women. I'm trying to find other sisters, because there may be 400 people in the senior management conference, and I want to feel "safe" by having sisters to talk to during breaks or lunch. It's always depressing when I see women account for less than 10 percent of the attendees.

For me, it's feeling like an outlier. I ask myself, *Do I deserve to be here?* Then, of course, I tell myself, *Of course I do. I've worked so hard to*

---

[25] KPMG Women's Leadership Study, Moving Women Forward into Leadership Roles, KPMG.com/WomensLeadership, https://home.kpmg/content/dam/kpmg/ph/pdf/ThoughtLeadershipPublications/KPMGWomensLeadershipStudy.pdf

[26] Kay, Kay, and Shipman, Claire, *The Confidence Code: The Science and Art of Self-Assurance—What Women Should Know*, HarperBusiness, 2014.

get here. Then the next thing that comes to mind is, *Okay, well, I need to prove my value.* We put this pressure on ourselves, and I'm not sure men think like that as much as we do. They don't count the number of men there because it is obvious they are the majority. As Michael Kimmel said, "Privilege is invisible to those who have it." He goes on to say, "So making gender visible to men is the first step to engaging men to support gender equality."

We need more role models who we are inspired by and want to emulate and aspire to be. The KPMG study[27] found that 86 percent of women said, "When I see women in leadership, I am encouraged that I can get there myself." It is a Catch-22 situation because we need more women in leadership to encourage other women, but the challenge is getting the women to leadership positions to begin with.

One of the ways of increasing the number of women in leadership is to encourage each other as sisters. This means that if you are a woman in leadership, you need to set the right example and mentor women more junior than you. I know that many of you are very busy and don't have the capacity to mentor, but unless we make the effort, things won't change for any of us. We have to work together to break this cycle.

---

[27] KPMG Women's Leadership Study, Moving Women Forward into Leadership Roles, KPMG.com

Chapter 3

Why do We Need Sisterhood in the Workplace?

In investment banking, there were so many gossip mills and rumors about women. "Oh, that woman must be sleeping with that guy. They have a very close relationship." It's quite frustrating. As I mentioned in the last chapter, if a woman is succeeding and is supported by a male mentor or sponsor in the process, a lot of women (and men) will think, "Oh, there's gotta be something there." When I left banking, there were rumors that I left because I had an affair with my boss, which is ridiculous, and I was very upset about it.

I left because there was no more upside for me in that company. I'd made it to the top, and there weren't any areas of growth for me in that job, so I decided to try being an entrepreneur. But I felt that all my years at that company, and everything I'd done, was undermined by that rumor. I was disheartened, and kept wondering why they thought that. *The only reason I could think of was that I'm a woman.*

Enter sisterhood. We can be the ones who stop the gossiping, rather than adding fuel to the fire; otherwise, it will be difficult for women to succeed.

Based on numerous studies—especially in law and banking—women suffer in the corporate setting for jobs well done because other women undermine their accomplishments. How many of you have heard countless stories or been subject to being backstabbed by another woman following an accomplishment, or had to deal with an extremely difficult, competitive woman who makes your job harder to do? According to a 2007 survey from the Employment Law Alliance, of the 45 percent of people who said they had been bullied in the workplace, 40 percent said they were bullied by women. That in and of itself does not prove that women are more likely to torment other women. But a 2014 report from the Workplace Bullying Institute claims that women who were considered workplace bullies targeted other women 68 percent of the time. A survey from 2011 found that 95 percent of female respondents had cited at least one instance of being undercut by another woman in the workplace.[1]

Some of you will be thinking, *this doesn't apply to me* or *I have never witnessed this*, and that's fine. But please recognize that the point of this book is to get us to think about these topics and ask ourselves if we can do better. I also know that there are plenty of men who sabotage women and hold us back. But right now I want to focus on what we, as sisters, can do better.

Female Colleagues Hold Each Other Back

Whether we receive criticism or backlash from other women, it is apparent that, too often, we see ourselves as the competition, rather than a united group that strives for women as a whole who deserve respect, support, and understanding from each other. When doing so, however, we create even more competition for ourselves—competition that could actually be much-needed support that would benefit all of us. That is why I point to the woman vs. woman competition as unhealthy.

---

[1] Strauss, Karsten, Women in the Workplace: Are Women Tougher on Other Women? Forbes.com, Jul 18, 2016,

Unhealthy Competition

Women have to deal with more unhealthy competition in the workplace than their male counterparts. Why? I think it is because there are so few women at the top, and, therefore, we really do have to compete with each other to make it. If you know that only one of ten in a group of women are going to make it, you're definitely going to look at the other nine and compare yourself to them to determine if you're the one who could make it.

Even unconsciously, I think this competition affects the way you behave. Studies show that women are less supportive of other women in conditions where they are both under-represented in the workplace and feel there are only a few opportunities for advancement. Therefore, we end up competing with one another, instead of helping one another up.

Other studies have shown that women in male-dominated firms distance themselves from other women when there appears to be few opportunities for women because those women view their gender as an impediment. They avoid joining forces and sometimes turn on one another.

"Women, rather than building each other up and helping—sometimes we tear each other down," Gabriel, an assistant professor of management and organizations at the University of Arizona, told *Today*. One part of it is that women often view other women as their competition at work, Gabriel said: "So rather than me comparing myself to my male counterparts when it comes to things like raises or promotions, I'm more likely to compare myself to other women."[2]

You can't have sisterhood if there's rivalry based on a scarcity mentality. I think that really unravels healthy competition—you want your sister to succeed, but if you have this unhealthy competitive

---

[2] Pawlowski, A., Why Women are Rude to Each Other and How to Deal, Today. com, Mar. 2018, https://www.today.com/health/work-incivility-women-report-more-rudeness-other-women-t124262

mindset, it's so much harder to develop strong business relationships with female co-workers.

I was mentoring a woman in investment banking and trying to bring her up the ladder. When she became more senior, I noticed her behavior changed. She started saying negative things about the women who were junior to her. I don't think she would say to herself, *Oh, I'm competitive*, but I do think the intimidation of other women who she perceived as "better" was threatening to her. When she heard someone say that a certain female coworker was doing an amazing job, she didn't agree or go along with the compliment. Instead, I think she felt that need to compete and withheld positive agreement.

As mentioned in Chapter 1, research shows that some of this can be traced to our DNA and also our childhood.

In an article titled "Competition Among Women: Myth and Reality," Dr. Lynn Margolies, a Harvard Medical School Psychologist, writes that there is a difference between men and women in how they approach social competition. From a young age, boys are encouraged to be confident and to engage in healthy competition (e.g., sports, debate, video gaming, etc.). On the other hand, confidence and healthy competition can be viewed as "undesirable traits" in young girls (e.g., dubbing a young, active girl a "tomboy").[3]

As a result, men view winning as an essential part of the game, do not feel bad for those who don't win, and are able to maintain camaraderie with their co-competitors. In short, friendship and competition remain very distinct. Women learn that they are not supposed to be competitive and should not win at the expense of others. As such, natural competitive tendencies cannot be channeled

---

[3] Margolies, Lynn Ph.D, Competition Among Women: Myth and Reality, Oct. 2018, Psych Central, Competition Among Women, Myth and Reality, http://psychcentral. com/lib/competition-among-women-myth-and-reality/

in a healthy manner and fester as secret feelings of envy and desire to see another woman fail, all "laced with guilt and shame."

There's always going to be competition, whether among men or women. Generally speaking, men will view other men as competition as part of the job and in terms of performance, results, and revenue or income. They're not accusing men of sleeping their way to the top, shaming them about their choice of tie, or saying they're too sexy, too thin, or too fat behind their backs (at least I don't see it as overtly as I do with women). Women compete on a much more personal level and say or do things that can be so hurtful.

QUEEN BEE SYNDROME

The concept of queen bee syndrome first came to light in the 1970s. A 1974 study found that women who were successful in male-dominated industries were sometimes capable of hindering the progress of other women in the workplace. Studies found that women who achieved success in male-dominated environments felt threatened by other women, which made them more likely to oppose the rise of other women. Some of the "queen bee" mentality is that since they suffered, so should other women.

I know a lot of people may say, "Oh, this queen bee thing doesn't exist." I totally disagree with that, because I've seen it.

When I was up for Managing Director (MD), I asked one of the female Managing Directors I worked with if she would be supportive of me because I knew the support of other MDs was necessary to make MD. She said, "Yes, of course." Then, when I didn't make it the first time, I asked my boss whether that particular woman was supportive, and he said that she didn't say a word to help my chances. The second time I was put up for promotion, I decided not to ask her because I knew she didn't support me at all. I got the promotion.

A recent research from the University of Arizona suggest that the problem may be getting worse, finding that women experience a higher level of rudeness from other female colleagues than they do from male colleagues. Allison Gabriel, assistant professor of management and organizations at the University of Arizona's Eller College of Management, said, "Women are ruder to each other than they are to men, or than men are to women."

When transitioning from employee to employer, women face having to become detached from former female friendships in the office and risk being seen as a "dragon lady" almost immediately. "There is a chance queen bees are mean to junior female employees because they want to distance themselves from other women," states psychologist and UCLA lecturer Kim Elsesser. "Since women often face discrimination and don't have the same opportunities at work as men do, queen bees think they will have better opportunities if they are perceived as one of the guys. Therefore, the bees are reluctant to help other women because they don't want to call attention to their own gender."[4]

Having a queen bee attitude can run the risk of more women leaving the workforce because of the frustrations they face when dealing with these "queen bees." In one of the organizations that I joined, there was a senior woman whose comments had me crying a few times. She wasn't very friendly and, in fact, was quite nasty to me. When I first joined, she made me feel like an outsider. She was one of those "mean girls." I went to some of the senior men and asked them what I should do, and they said, "Yeah, she's not very nice to you. Just ignore her."

Although I tried my best to befriend her (I would try to make conversation, give her a compliment, or ask for her views), I realized that she just didn't like the fact that I was part of senior management. Nothing that I did would make her like me. I was tempted to quit

---

[4] Sharkey Lauren, Evolution or sexism: Why are so many female bosses 'queen bees'? Metro.co.uk, May, 2018, https://metro.co.uk/2018/05/24/evolution-or-sexism-why-are-so-many-female-bosses-queen-bees-7548191/

my job because I didn't want to work with someone like her, but in the end, I decided to ignore her and persevere. However, according to Allison Gabriel, "evidence emerged in the three studies that companies may face a greater risk of losing female employees who experience female-instigated incivility, as they reported less satisfaction at work and increased intentions to quit their current jobs in response to these unpleasant experiences."[5]

I've seen it in other situations, when senior women won't have coffee with a junior because she doesn't have time, or she doesn't want to help for whatever reason. But these same women were members of "women's empowerment industry groups" – so they seem to be supportive, when, in fact, they are not.

Again, it seems that as women become more senior and, therefore, see fewer women at the top, women tend to want to be the one who stays there . . . unchecked by other female coworkers. Although this queen bee mentality does not apply to many senior women, it still exists and given the lack of women at the top, we can't afford to have *any* senior women have this mentality. The queen bees must stop because they prevent other talented, up-and-coming women from advancing in the workplace.[6]

WOMEN AS MEAN GIRLS

There are too many TV shows and movies to list that portray women who are authoritative and know what they want as being wicked. That type of stereotype is very painful and can be internalized by young and impressionable women. We talked about *The Devil Wears Prada* and

---

[5] Incivility at Work: Is 'Queen Bee Syndrome' Getting Worse?, University of Arizona, UA News, Feb. 2018, https://uanews.arizona.edu/story/incivility-work-queen-bee-syndrome-getting-worse

[6] Harvey, Cecilia, "Queen bees" hinder women in the workplace, ICAEW.com, Apr. 2018, https://economia.icaew.com/opinion/april-2018/queen-bees-hinder-women-in-the-workplace

Working Girl in the introduction to this book. These successful women are portrayed as demonic, selfish, and cruel, and unfortunately our society and the writers in Hollywood tend to support such stereotyping. That doesn't help. Why does Cinderella have the evil stepmom? You rarely have movies that portray an evil stepdad.

Women also feed into that stereotype for ratings or attention. I have nieces who are teenagers, and they'd watch *The Bachelor, The Bachelorette, Jersey Shore, Love Island* or any version of *The Real Housewives of (Pick a City)*. These women are extremely catty, callous, and vicious with each other . . . and these are women who are supposed to be friends! When my nieces or anyone's children see that, they also feed into and engage with that type of stereotyping for entertainment. It becomes acceptable or even *expected* behavior for women. Every girl knows about cliques of girls who are in the popular crowd. It's much more noticeable to girls who's in the popular crowd and who's not. It becomes embedded in them that cat fights and girl fights are normal and okay.

How does all of this translate into the workplace? Our preconditioning and instincts are hard to shake, especially when we see myriad examples of it every day, whether on television and in the movies, on the playground, or in the office.

I find it interesting that my direct reports will tell me that people always ask them, "What's it like to work with Jaclyn?" I asked them why they ask this question and their response is always, "They want to know if you are difficult to work with." They said that people are curious because they know I work hard and am successful, so I must be very ambitious and a slave driver. I usually try to laugh this off, but honestly, if you think about it, *is it fair that I'm always being closely examined and scrutinized?* Why should successful women be immediately considered to be a bitch or slave driver? Why don't they ever ask what it is like to work with a male boss? People may deny that they scrutinize women leaders more than men, but I will tell you that it happens all the time.

There was a senior man who was my peer, and he wasn't a good boss. He was one of those guys who was excellent at managing up but not good with peers or subordinates, but they never questioned him or the way he led (even though people complained about him); however, they certainly looked at whether I got along with others. In fact, I felt as if I were under the microscope *all the time*. It was frustrating and unfair, but the men who were scrutinizing me didn't realize the double standard that they were applying.

WOMEN WHO PREFER MALE BOSSES

I've asked some of my female mentees, and almost all of them said they prefer a male boss because women tend to be more difficult and bossy. Men are perceived to be more laid back—they're easier and they're not micro-managers. But I don't think these mentees understand that the female bosses I've seen work faster, harder, and micromanage to try to get things done because they want to get home and spend time with their family. Male bosses don't mind going on business trips, and they don't mind going for a drink after work. As a working mom, we have a limited amount of time at work, so we have to be as productive and diligent as possible so we can get home to deal with a million other things. So, colleagues easily assume we're just not as friendly when we don't go out for drinks after work. I view it as working moms trying to be protective of the limited time we have to spend at home with our families.

When my kids were younger, I was constantly thinking, *Okay, how do I get home in time?* The answer to that question was always, *Work fast, make sure people are on task, and let me do my job.* So, did I micromanage? Maybe. Did I spend less time being social? Absolutely. Did that mean I didn't care about the team? Absolutely not.

But I will say this, it gets easier as your children get older. Now that my kids are in college, I can travel a lot more and be more social at work. I can also step out of my office and say, "Hey guys, want to have a drink?" But it certainly took a long time to get to this point.

But if most women think like my mentees, then how are we going to get more women in senior positions if we don't want to work for other women and women fuel the misconceptions and stereotypes by calling senior women "bossy, difficult, dragon lady, or bitchy?" Some of them have never even worked for a woman! When a manager hears female colleagues saying they don't want to work for a woman for these stereotypical reasons, don't you think that male managers might think twice before promoting a female?

Like the mentees that I've asked, studies have shown that when asked, women will say that they prefer a male boss over a female, whereas men are indifferent. A 2014 Gallup poll in the U.S. found women were more likely than men to want a male boss. Only one-fifth of people surveyed said they preferred a female boss over a man. In fact, in the 60 years that Gallup has conducted this survey, women have never preferred a female boss . . . until only last year. The percentage of American women preferring a male boss is at a historical low of 27 percent, a 12-point drop from 2014.[7]

Though favor toward a male boss experienced the greatest decrease over the past six decades, favor toward a female boss has seen very little increase—28 percent in 2017, whereas it was 25 percent in 2014. Even in the UK, in a similar survey, the message was clear that women are less likely than men to want a woman boss. A OnePoll survey of 2,000 female full- and part-time employees revealed that almost two-thirds (63 percent) prefer to have a man as their immediate line-manager. Men were seen to be 'more authoritative,' 'more straight-talking,' and less prone to mood swings than their female counterparts. Women

---

[7] Brenan, Megan, Americans No Longer Prefer Male Boss to Female Boss, Gallup, Nov. 2017, https://news.gallup.com/poll/222425/americans-no-longer-prefer-male-boss-female-boss.aspx

also felt that female managers were likely to feel more threatened by other managers, failed to leave personal problems at home, and were less flexible on the issue of starting and leaving times.[8]

Why, as women, wouldn't we just say that we don't have a preference?

As we all know, there are not that many women in power. Interestingly, in these Gallup polls, a majority of people who said they prefer a male boss had never had a female one.

> With such a small sample to go on, we look at each woman under a microscope, each gesture indicative of the quality of every single female boss from now until forever. If a man's a bad boss, it's because he's a jerk. But if a woman's a bad boss? It's because she's a woman. The fact that pollsters ask this question seems like part of the problem. So just because polls show people prefer a male boss doesn't mean women are *actually worse bosses*. In the poll, people who did have female bosses preferred them! But it doesn't really matter if women can be great bosses if we're saying the opposite so often and so loudly. If women are perceived as lesser bosses, that affects your chances of ever becoming one.[9]

Laurie Rudman, a social psychologist at Rutgers University, conducted research to learn why it isn't accepted for women to behave in the same manner as men. She found a psychological concept called "system justification" to be one reason. Translated, system justification happens when historically oppressed groups (in this case, women) observe or experience unfairness and internalize any resulting negative stereotypes. In other words, they accept the norm as their default. When asked who they want to work with, they are likely to say a man.

---

[8] Ri5.co.uk, Two-thirds of Women Prefer Male Bosses, August, 2009, https://www.ri5.co.uk/site/news/article/twothirds-of-women-prefer-male-bosses/

[9] Why are We So Hard on Women Bosses? Cosmopolitan.com, Mar. 2018, https://www.cosmopolitan.com/career/advice/a5872/women-bosses/

After all, there aren't as many female managers and leaders, so men must be better.[10]

As mentioned, the good news is that this preference by women for male bosses seem to be changing. For the first time since 1953, Americans no longer prefer a male boss over a female boss, according to a recent Gallup poll findings in 2017. The Gallup poll surveyed 1,028 adults, and 44 percent of the women said it did not matter to them if their manager was male or female. That's up from 34 percent in 2014. Men who didn't have a preference also increased, from 58 percent to 68 percent in 2017. This poll shows that women are more likely to have a preference than men, and up till this year that preference used to be for a male boss.

Given that this poll was conducted after multiple women and men had accused powerful men like Harvey Weinstein and Kevin Spacey of sexual harassment and assault, it is possible that this affected the poll, but hopefully this trend will continue.

Rather than saying that gender of the leader matters, we should continue to say that it doesn't matter. What matters is how effective and how good that person is as a leader. Before you decide whether or not you dislike having a female boss, ask yourself if you've had enough female bosses to really assess what female bosses are like. If you really hate your female boss, is it because she is a woman (i.e., are you holding your female boss to the same standards that you would expect of a man)? Female bosses are expected to do a lot more than their male counterparts; are you giving her a fair chance?

Women Unsupportive Of Successful Women

Women aren't always the best employees to other women, either. Female subordinates can show less respect and deference to female bosses than

---

[10] Khazan, Olga, Why do Women Bully Each Other at Work, *The Atlantic*, Sept. 2017, https://www.theatlantic.com/magazine/archive/2017/09/the-queen-bee-in-the-corner-office/534213/

to their male bosses. When I started my current job, it was a woman who asked me, "Why did you come back to finance when you don't have to work?" The woman who asked me this is part of a Women's Leadership Group. I was surprised that, rather than being supportive of my new role, she was questioning why I was even doing it!

Could it be due to envy? According to Joyce Benenson, in her book *Warriors and Worriers*, women compete with unrelated women, and in order to protect ourselves from attack by other women, we need to be "nice" and not discuss personal success with other women. Instead of speaking of their many achievements, successful women should focus on their weaknesses instead. "A woman who states that she attained exactly the goal she was striving for is taking a big risk. Other women would feel extremely envious. Envious females might attempt to ruin a woman's success by socially excluding her. Better to maintain that all women are equal and that lucky outcomes are outside one's control. Best never to mention personal success at all. Only when a girl or woman feels she is failing can she speak freely. Other females are truly sympathetic. They can afford to be because they are ahead."[11]

Perhaps this is why some women just don't want to see other women succeed. I have seen situations where a man was gunning for a senior position, and his guy pals would all be very supportive and vocal for his promotion. However, when I've asked women to do the same for another woman, they just weren't very enthusiastic. Most say it is because they don't think that they have any influence to help the other, but I sometimes wonder if it is because they don't necessarily want to see a woman succeed or perhaps they don't like to see another woman being so assertive by gunning for a senior position.

We all know that if a man is gunning for a role, it's just him being competitive and assertive. But if a woman is gunning for the same role, both men and women say and think, *wow, she's really aggressive . . .* or

---

[11] Benenson, Joyce, *Warriors and Worriers*, page 176

why does she think she should get the job? It's viewed differently. Of course, there's the simplistic line of thinking that her behavior goes against the grain of being feminine. So, if a woman overtly says, "I want to be the CEO," it's rare that she's going to have a group of female co-workers or leaders rally around her. More often, female colleagues will think, *who does she think she is . . . why does she think she's going to make it?* And then suddenly the back talk starts with all the behind-the-scenes maliciousness. Whereas if a man says, "Yeah, I'm going to be the CEO," we think he's ambitious and on a career track.

So, instead of using stereotypes to diminish our female colleagues, what if we became the ones to say positive things about our fellow women leaders? I suspect if managers heard more of that, it would mean more women would be supported in getting to the top and with a lot less drama and unnecessary hardship.

Unrealistically High Expectations Of Female Bosses

Many women set unrealistically high standards and expectations for female managers. Research reveals that women expect more from a relationship with female leaders. Women's relational expectations of female leaders include their building connection and trust through sharing and listening. Women expect more flexibility, emotional understanding, and support from female bosses than they do from male bosses, and female bosses who do not focus on relationship building can be seen "very negatively" by their female staff.[12]

We expect leaders to be ambitious, confident, and driven, not caring or sensitive. Therefore, men are automatically at a leadership advantage because their behaviour is consistent with perceptions. In contrast, if women are expected to focus on relationships, they are

---

[12] Loren, Anna, Women Hold Female Bosses to Higher Emotional Standard than Male Bosses – Study, Stuff.co.nz, June 2017, https://www.stuff.co.nz/business/93863996/women-hold-female-bosses-to-higher-emotional-standard—study

perceived to be likeable but weak (not leadership material). However, if they exhibit the assertive behaviours leaders are expected to possess, they are in violation of their gender-role stereotypes and are perceived to be unlikable, self-interested, and bitchy (and, therefore, not leadership material).

Imagine the challenges that women face given this backdrop. Because women are stereotyped as the nurturers, it means that, when they're at work, they are expected to be kind, sweet, soft spoken, sympathetic, and empathetic . . . all while trying to do her job or manage a team or an entire department at the time. And if you're not the nurturer and really just want to focus on getting your work done, you're likely to be categorized as being difficult, bitchy, or unfriendly because it's going against the grain of the expectation that you should be feminine and nurturing.

For example, if I'm very busy and don't have time that day to socialize with the team, people will say something like, "Oh my gosh, is something wrong? Why are you in such a bad mood?" I don't hear women complaining about a male boss not chatting with them enough. They don't have to. My only behavior is trying to focus on getting my work done. Whereas, I don't see that standard applying at all to men. I've had male bosses who don't spend any time with the staff. In fact, when I asked one of my bosses if he wanted to meet new incoming analysts who were fresh out of grad school, he said, "No, I don't; what's the point? If things go bad, we're going to have to fire them, so I'd rather not get to know them."

I know a lot of men who don't want to spend time with staff, and that's okay. But if a woman was like that, she would be labeled as cold, not very nice, or worse. These double standards are tough. I want to get my work done, and I just want to go home and see my children and be able to clock out by 7:00 pm. So, on some busy days, I don't have time to socialize with people. That doesn't mean I'm not in a good mood; I just have a lot of work to do so I can get home! But, like I said, that same type of expectation is not there for men. No one says, "Oh, why is that guy not spending time talking to me?" when they see him focusing on work.

Another double standard is the way you have to "be" in the office. It's a constant battle to think about how I am in the office. For example, I have to think about my tone and the way I'm delivering a message. I usually have to ask myself, *Am I coming across too authoritative? Am I being friendly enough?* Even if I try my best to soften my tone, it doesn't matter. They're going to label me that way, anyway. I often crack jokes because I like humor in the office, but regardless, my boss told me that I need to smile more. (This from a boss who *never* smiles or cracks any jokes.)

There's a balancing act a woman must do all the time that I don't think men experience. In addition to watching our tone, we don't want to talk too much or not talk at all. We must watch our mannerisms— *am I folding my arms too much?* We don't want to frown or smile too much, either. We always have to be careful that we don't do things where people will then label us, *"Oh my gosh, she is such a bitch. She's so evil. She's so difficult. She's so aggressive."*

In *See Jane Lead*, (Business Plus, 2007), Lois P. Frankel, Ph.D. writes that "the tendency for people to rely on gender stereotypes to define successful leadership in organizations emerges across different national contexts and cultures worldwide (Schein, Mueller, Lituchy, & Liu, 1996). Whereas male leadership is generally expected to be characterized by a focus on task achievement and performance outcomes indicating competence (characteristic for transactional leadership), people expect female leaders to focus on interpersonal relations and work satisfaction characteristic of interpersonal warmth (associated with transformational leadership; Bass, 1985; Bass & Avolio, 1990; see also Williams & Best, 1990)."

The Center for Creative Leadership's White Paper found that traditional stereotypes of leaders, such as being assertive, having authority, and taking initiative are misidentified as typically "male traits." When women take the lead and assert ourselves, we could be perceived as aggressive, emotional, or irrational. Ambitious men are seen as natural and unremarkable. But when women is ambitious, it's shocking, offensive, and selfish.

So, women who want to advance their careers often find themselves in a quagmire.

- Women leaders are "damned if they do, doomed if they don't."

- Women leaders are perceived as either competent or liked, but difficult to be both.

- Women leaders are considered bossy if they are assertive, but they are ignored if they don't assert themselves.

For women to succeed, they have to be different, extraordinary, and not too emotional. But for them to be respected by their female employees, it seems these women also need to be relatable, likable, and "just like everyone else." When they're not, there's major backlash. Men are continually applauded for being ambitious, powerful, and successful, but women who display these same traits often pay a social penalty. No wonder there are not more women at the top—it is exhausting, given the expectations that they have to always strive to meet.

I'd like to envision how my "male bosses" would have fared if they were women instead of men, but had the same personality or behavior. One senior person I knew was a sycophant. He knew how to "manage up," but was not very good at managing down. He would go drinking with his male bosses almost every night—they are part of the "men's club." That person, if he were a woman, would probably be called a party girl (which is frowned upon) who must be sleeping with the boss. That "woman" would probably be fired.

Another senior male manager I knew was extremely difficult. He would lose his temper, expect everyone to work 24/7, and was the type of person who had to have the exact bullet style he wanted used in his presentations. If he were a woman, the words "dragon lady" or "micromanager" would have been bandied about, and "she" would have been fired. Another senior male manager I knew had a very short attention span and hardly ever said anything positive about anyone—*ever*. If he were a woman, the headwinds would be strong, and "she'd" be out. But all of them are still around and, in fact, doing fine. They don't have the pressures of needing to be "nice." Just generate the revenue, and that is enough to let them get by for most male managers.

There is also this expectation by women that other women need to be "nice." As Sheryl Sandberg, Facebook's chief operating officer, observed in 2018: "Women aren't any meaner to women than men are to one another. Women are just expected to be nicer."[13] In *Lean In*, Sharon Meers addressed this issue with Sheryl Sandberg, saying that "both men and women do, in fact, demand more time and warmth from women in the workplace. We expect greater niceness from women and can become angry when they don't conform to that expectation."[14]

In speaking with Professor Gruenfeld for *Lean In*, Gruenfeld explained the price women pay for success. "Our entrenched cultural ideas associate men with leadership qualities and women with nurturing qualities and put women in a double bind," she said. "We believe not only that women are nurturing, but that they *should be* nurturing above all else. When a woman does anything that signals she might not be nice first and foremost, it creates a negative impression and makes us uncomfortable."[15]

---

[13] BBC Team, Queen bees: Do women hinder the progress of other women?, BBC.com, Jan. 2018, https://www.bbc.com/news/uk-41165076

[14] *Lean In*, Page 166

[15] *Lean In*, Page 43

Part of this can probably be again due to our DNA. Most girls and women expect other girls and women to be nice. So, women are genuinely perplexed when another woman isn't nice. In one of Joyce Benenson's studies, she asked pre-adolescent children to describe each of their same-sex classmates. Almost every girl judged the other girls in her class in terms of their "niceness." It was the most important quality when describing the other females in the class. Boys were less interested in others' niceness; rather, they focused on the skills of their male classmates.[16]

This expectation of being "nice" flows into the workplace. If a woman is not nice, then there is retaliation by other women in the office.

Do successful women have an obligation to be liked? No more so than successful men. Nor do they have a responsibility to represent all women, or even some women. As we look at the rise of females in charge, there's been speculation of a future of kinder, gentler work environments. Maybe that will happen, maybe it won't. But guaranteed, the onus isn't on the queen bee alone. It's on her worker bees as well.

NOW WHAT?

As I, and now you, my sister, read through the list of problems in the workplace that are exclusive to women, it can seem overwhelming and more than a little depressing. But it's not insurmountable. We can turn this around. The chapters that follow will show the way to do it.

---

[16] *Warriors and Worriers*, page 175

Chapter 4

Women as Bosses and Leaders

In addition to the reasons I laid out in Chapter 2 on why there are so few women at the top, could one of the reasons be that women just don't make good leaders? The answer is a resounding NO. In fact, it's been well documented that women have more of the required leadership traits than men in a variety of formats . . . whether in categories of initiative and clear communication, openness and ability to innovate, or goal setting. Many of our amazing gender predilections give us an advantage over our male counterparts.[1]

If you haven't seen Tomas Chamorro-Premuzic's TED Talk titled "Why Do So Many Incompetent Men Become Leaders?", you should watch it. He argues that, based on research on the psychology of leadership, if leaders were selected on competence rather than confidence; humility rather than charisma; and integrity rather than narcissism, we would not just end up with more competent leaders, but also more women leaders. His studies show that most of the leaders today (who are men) are incompetent.

Why are there so many incompetent men who *become* leaders?

---

[1] Hosie, Rachel, Women are Better Leaders than Men, Study of 3,000 Managers Concludes, Independent.co.uk, Sept. 2017 https://www.independent.co.uk/life-style/women-better-leaders-men-study-a7658781.html

Based on his findings, he argues that there are three main reasons: first, when looking for a leader, we are not good at distinguishing between confidence (how good people think they are) and competence (how good they actually are); second, we love charismatic leaders (the best leaders are humble to the point that they are boring); and third, we gravitate toward narcissists. Many of these male leaders lack empathy and self-control because they are unaware of their limitations.

The best leaders care about other people and spend time worrying about their reputation. We should focus on the right traits, qualities that make better leaders—leaders who promote competency, humility, and integrity. If we insisted on these qualities, we would have more female than male leaders since women score higher than men on these three traits.

He goes on to say that we should stop expecting women to act like incompetent men; it also means not ruling out men who do not have the traditional "masculine" traits.[2]

THE INHERENT "MALE BOSS" ADVANTAGES

Not only do men have the advantage that women usually prefer to work for them, but they also have many other advantages because of the fact that almost all of the top positions are held by men. Men don't have to worry about going for a drink or dinner with their male boss; they can build a friendship with their male bosses outside of work more easily than women peers, and they don't have to worry about any gossip; they don't have to worry about how they look or what they are wearing; their mentors/sponsors are usually men with influence who can help them; they don't have to worry about negative stereotypes and they don't have to worry about whether they are being too "bossy" or "bitchy."

When men walk into a room, they're assumed to be competent until they reveal otherwise. For women, it's the other way around. We

---

[2] Chamorro-Premuzic, Tomas, "Why so many incompetent men become leaders?", TED Talk, https://m.youtube.com/watch?v=zeAEFEXvcBg

have to constantly prove that we are competent. Men are not expected to be nice, either. They can be aggressive, and that's fine. For women, we pay a heavy penalty if we act as aggressively as men.

In Michael Kimmel's TED Talk on "Why Gender Equality is Good for Everyone - Men Included", he provides a great summary of why we need gender equality in the workplace, in a very entertaining way. I love this statement by Michael in his TED Talk, ". . . white men in Europe and the United States are the beneficiaries of the single greatest affirmative action program in the history of the world. It is called 'the history of the world.'"[3]

Gender inequality is nothing new. From the time of birth, boys and girls are conditioned to follow gender suit. Girls are gifted dolls so they can make believe they are mothers, and boys are gifted trucks so they can do "man's" work. This is as true today as it was in the mid 20th century. We live and function in a primarily patriarchal society, and the remnants of the past conditioning replays itself with every generation.

Yes, women become mothers, and men become fathers. But the line has grayed in other gender roles. Women are no longer just homemakers. Their careers have expanded from teaching and nursing, and females today are lawyers, doctors, administrators, architects, and, while it is less common, women are proving themselves to be effective scientists, carpenters, engineers, and mathematicians.

Unfortunately, the conditioning that determines our life and career paths begins at a young age. Boys are taught how to use power tools with their fathers, while girls are taught how to set tables and do dishes with their mothers. Well-meaning parents even discourage boys from participating in "feminine" tasks, just as they protect their daughters

---

[3] Kimmel, Michael, TED Talk, "Why Gender Equality is Good for Everyone—Men Included" https://www.ted.com/talks/michael_kimmel_why_gender_equality_is_good_for_everyone_men_included/transcript?language=en

from doing physical labor like learning how to start a lawn mower, maintain an automobile, or build a treehouse.

A 2014 Verizon advertisement entitled "Inspire Her Mind" exemplifies this conditioning as it depicts a girl being discouraged from participating in the creation of a science fair project in favor of her more capable brother. Saying that it's time we let our daughters know that they can be pretty and "pretty brilliant," the ad shares that only 18 percent of engineering majors are girls.[4]

Most certainly, this conditioning also results in fewer girls choosing careers in science, technology, and math, as well as senior level management. Not only is this conditioning related to toys, hobbies, and studies, but it also extends to extracurricular activities, specifically sports. In fact, studies have shown that men play organized and competitive sports, while women tend to participate in sports for the health and social benefits they receive. Not only are girls conditioned to play sports for different reasons than boys, but they perceive those sports differently—males are more likely to include sports as an accomplishment or skill on a CV or resume, while females would qualify it as a hobby.

Jodie Skellern, PhD candidate at Macquarie University and a former AMP executive, found that participation in organized and competitive sports correlates to higher achievement at work. According to Skellern, sports at that level provides "resilience and teamwork, all translate very easily into a competitive advantage for men that leads to high achievement in the workplace." In a July, 2016, HRM.com article by Clive Hopkins, she states, "A human resources director told me that even if a male has played division four sport, it plays a bigger role in his life and he'll elevate this to a higher level. Women, though,

---

[4] Verizon commercial, Inspire Her Mind, 2014, YouTube.com, https://www.youtube.com/watch?v=XP3cyRRAfX0

often don't volunteer sport [as an achievement] unless they've played at the top level."[5]

Note, however, that Skellern is quick to state that sports, per se, might not be the reason that males who participate in competitive sports tend to advance further. Instead, she suggests that society just might be biased when selecting candidates for senior level positions and, on an unconscious level, those charged with such decisions may unconsciously perceive current or former male athletes are more qualified or capable.

In spite of our conditioning and obstacles, women still aspire to advance in their careers, at least at the onset. According to a Bain & Company study, women with under two years of work experience start out slightly more ambitious than men, but that hopefulness is quickly drained out of them. After two years, the average woman's aspirations and confidence plummet by 60 percent and 50 percent, respectively.[6]

Men, meanwhile, only experience a 10 percent drop, possibly because they see all their female colleagues losing interest in getting promoted and figure that it improves their odds. Senior managers of both genders fare better, but when it comes to upward mobility, men are almost twice as confident. Why the disparity? It's not due to women getting married and having kids. It seems to come down to workplace culture.

Senior management in the majority of companies consists of white men, and naturally, they reward and applaud the accomplishments of their male peers and subordinates. Initially, though, both men and women believe they have the success qualities their companies want, and they feel they have supervisors who support their career goals.

---

[5] Hopkins, Clive, HRMonline.com, Men Have a Competitive Advantage in the Workplace. Here's Why, https://www.hrmonline.com.au/section/featured/men-competitive-advantage-workplace/

[6] Gadiesh, Orit and Coffman, Julie, Companies Drain Women's Ambition After Only 2 Years, HBR.com, May 2015, https://hbr.org/2015/05/companies-drain-womens-ambition-after-only-2-years

However, those feelings are not sustained over time for women, who believe that original support has declined. Men, on the contrary, do not witness a similar decline in support.

Of course, women are given other reasons for their lack of advancement—some are told they're just not a good candidate or qualified enough, while others might hear that they aren't showing that they want to be advanced in the workplace. This lack of support is reflected in the fact that two-thirds of male supervisors admit that they are reluctant to provide career counseling to young female workers because it is likely to be a waste of time.[7]

Men feel supported by their male bosses much more than females because men have each other's backs, which puts them at an advantage. Men tend to become buddies with each other at the top (i.e., "the boys club"), so if another man wants to do something (even though it may not be the ideal thing to do), they'll be more likely to be supportive because they're buddies. I see that in board meetings, too. Guys will say, "Yeah, yeah, of course, I support what he wants," because they are friends. So, they're definitely wired to support their teammates. This is exactly why we need to have diversity in the boardroom!

THE INHERENT "FEMALE BOSS" ADVANTAGES

The advantages are many, and they're backed by research and data.

In his TED Talk, Michael Kimmel states that men have a vested interested in making sure there is gender equality. "Not only does it make it happier for their wives and themselves, but gender equality is good for countries. It turns out, according to most studies, that those countries that are the most gender equal are also the countries that score highest on the happiness scale. It is also good for companies."

---

[7] Vail, Natalie, 5 Shockingly Outdated Problems Modern Women Face at Work, Cracked.com, Jan 2016, http://www.cracked.com/article_23372_5-hidden-pitfalls-being-woman-in-workplace.html

As Michael points out in his TED Talk, "Research by Catalyst and others has shown conclusively that the more gender-equal companies are, the better it is for workers, the happier their labor force is. They have lower job turnover. They have lower levels of attrition. They have an easier time recruiting. They have higher rates of retention, higher job satisfaction, higher rates of productivity. The question I'm often asked in companies is, "Boy, this gender equality thing, that's really going to be expensive, huh?" And I say, "Oh no, in fact, what you have to start calculating is how much gender inequality is already costing you. It is extremely expensive. So it is good for business."

Gender equality is a win-win situation for everyone. It is in the best interest of everyone.

In addition to the fact that having diversity is good for everyone, women just make better leaders. Based on our DNA, women have the ability to be hugely accomplished and successful. The book *Confidence Code* states, "Our brain structure means we like to get stuff right, make good judgements and hold bad impulses to a minimum. Our biological investment in emotions make us good at perceiving problems, at understanding the issues of others, and at moving forward reconciliations and solutions. And our highly integrated brain means we can take in large amounts of data and process it quickly."[8]

More Leadership Traits

In a May 2015 Bustle.com article, Melanie Kozak states, "It turns out that female employers are more likely to encourage employee development, check in on progress, provide positive feedback, set basic expectations for their employees, build relationships with their subordinates, encourage a positive team environment, and provide employees with opportunities to develop within their

---

[8] *The Confidence Code*, page 117

careers. I don't know about you, but these are definitely on my checklist for a good boss."[9]

In fact, as previously mentioned, the KPMG Women's Leadership Study[10] identified nine positive leadership behaviors exhibited by both male and female managers. The study found that we exhibit these behaviors with different frequencies. "Typically, female leaders use five leadership behaviors more often than their male counterparts: people development, expressing expectations and rewarding success, role-modeling, inspiration, and participative decision-making." The study concludes that women's leadership behaviors "help to improve companies' organizational performance by reinforcing five of the dimensions (vision, motivation, accountability, leadership, work environment, and values), and particularly the last three."

In McKinsey & Company's report of "Women Matter - Time to Accelerate," women and men equally apply intellectual stimulation and efficient communication, while men apply more individualistic decision making and control and corrective action. The leadership styles more frequently used by women are also considered to be the most effective in addressing the global challenges of the future. Four behaviors consistently emerged as being of particular importance for corporate performance over the next five years: "intellectual stimulation," "inspiration," "participative decision making," and "expectations and rewards."[11]

Recent research by the leadership consultancy Zenger Folkman supports this finding. According to Chief Operating Officer Robert

---

[9] Kozak, Melanie, Female Bosses Could Lead to More Engaged Employees at Work, Bustle.com, May 2015, https://www.bustle.com/articles/81980-female-bosses-could-lead-to-more-engaged-employees-at-work-says-gallup-poll-so-can-we

[10] KPMG Women's Leadership Study, page 14

[11] Women Matter: Time to Accelerate, McKinsey & Co., Oct. 2017, https://www.mckinsey.com/featured-insights/gender-equality/women-matter-ten-years-of-insights-on-gender-diversity/de-de

Sherwin, their study shows that women are actually more effective leaders than men, scoring higher on 12 of 16 leadership attributes.[12] In a *Harvard Business Review* study, where they conducted an analysis of thousands of 360-degree reviews, women outscored men on 17 of the 19 capabilities that differentiate excellent leaders from average or poor leaders. Women were rated as excelling in taking initiative, acting with resilience, practicing self-development, driving for results, and displaying high integrity and honesty.[13]

Not convinced yet? A Norwegian study found that women are better suited to be managers than men. The study, conducted by the BL Norwegian Business School, reviewed the traits of approximately 3,000 managers. Only five categories were studied, and women performed better than men in four of them: sociability and supportiveness; openness and ability to innovate; initiative and clear communication; and methodical management and goal setting. The one category where men outperformed women was emotional-related—particularly, that men deal with work stress better and are perceived to be more emotionally stable.[14]

WHY ARE WOMEN BETTER?

Because in order to succeed as a woman, we have to be. *Business Insider* published a 2014 article entitled, "Why Women are Better Leaders than Men." The author, Bob Sherwin, stated, "What do women do that creates this difference in leadership effectiveness? One of the clues

---

[12] Andersen, Erika, The Results are In: Women are Better Leaders, Forbes.com, https://www.forbes.com/sites/erikaandersen/2012/03/26/the-results-are-in-women-are-better-leaders/#758ff0336e03

[13] Zenger, Jack and Folkman, Joseph, Research: Women Score Higher Than Men in Most Leadership Skills Harvard Business Review, June 2019, https://hbr.org/2019/06/research-women-score-higher-than-men-in-most-leadership-skills

[14] Hosie, Rachel, Independent.com, March 2017, https://www.independent.co.uk/life-style/women-better-leaders-men-study-a7658781.html

for us came from talking with women about this research. When we ask them to explain why women were perceived as more effective, what we frequently heard was, "In order to get the same recognition and rewards, I need to do twice as much, never make a mistake and constantly demonstrate my competence."[15]

As quoted in Replicon.com, "Women make great leaders because the odds are against us to lead. When you're the underdog, it takes an extra push to get to the top. That's why the women who emerge on top are extraordinarily strong and capable. We had to fight to get there!" – Sarah Attman, principal, Sarah Rose Public Relations.[16]

Better Engagement and Teamwork

In 2015, a Gallup Poll found that 41 percent of female managers were engaged at work, compared with 35 percent of male managers, which likely results in more engaged, higher-performing teams.[17] According to the report, employees who work for a female manager are 1.26 times more likely than those who work for a male boss to strongly agree that "[t]here is someone at work who encourages my development." This suggests that female managers likely surpass their male counterparts in cultivating potential in others and helping to define a bright future for their employees. These findings could signify that women are more apt than men to find stimulating tasks to challenge their employees thus ensuring associates develop within their current roles and beyond.[18]

---

[15] Sherwin, Bob, Business Insider, Why Women are More Effective Leaders than Men, January 2014, https://www.businessinsider.com/study-women-are-better-leaders-2014-1

[16] 17 Reasons Women Make Great Leaders, Replicon.com, https://www.replicon.com/17-reasons-women-make-great-leaders/amp/

[17] Kozak, Melanie, Female Bosses Could Lead to More Engaged Employees at Work, Bustle.com

[18] Smith, Jacquelyn, Study Finds Women are Better Bosses than Men—Here's Why, Business Insider, Apr 2015, https://www.businessinsider.com/why-women-are-better-managers-than-men-2015-4

If female managers, on average, are more engaged than male managers, it stands to reason that they are likely to contribute more to their organization's current and future success.

Gallup provides further support. Employees who work for a female manager are six percentage points more engaged, on average, than those who work for a male manager—33 percent to 27 percent, respectively. Female employees who work for a female manager are the most engaged, at 35 percent. Male employees who report to a male manager are the least engaged, at 25 percent—a difference of 10 points."[19]

In addition to more engagement, women are better at creating a team building atmosphere. The feedback and open communication provided by female leaders provide an atmosphere that encourages employees to bond and create workplace friendships. Consequently, employees are better team players.

As quoted in Replicon.com's article, "17 Reasons Women Make Good Leaders," Katharine Nohr, principal, Nohr Sports Risk Management, states, "The women [I've worked with] consistently demonstrate passion, enthusiasm and an immense capacity to serve and be served by others. I've observed women make bold and wise decisions as leaders while relying on others to be part of their team. The environment is less authoritarian and more cooperative and family-like, but with solid leadership."[20]

Better Support For Career Development

In a joint study by the Center for Creative Leadership and Watermark in 2017, people with female bosses reported that their bosses were more supportive of their career development compared to people with

---

[19] Fitch, Kimberly and Agrawal, Sangeeta, Female Bosses are More Engaging than Males Bosses, Gallup.com, May, 2015, https://news.gallup.com/businessjournal/183026/female-bosses-engaging-male-bosses.aspx

[20] Replicon, 17 Reasons Women Make Great Leaders, https://www.replicon.com/17-reasons-women-make-great-leaders/amp/

male bosses. In fact, men and women with female bosses felt that the company at large was more committed to their career development. By putting women in leadership positions, it could help more employees feel supported, engaged, and less burned out.

Since women tend to be more natural nurturers (and not in terms of stereotypical expectations and extremes) than men, I think we do care more about the development of the team. When it comes to performance evaluations, my observation is that women take that very seriously. They know words matter. I will always have one-to-one reviews with my direct reports and spend time talking to them about what they've done well and areas for improvement. Many men I know feel that it is a waste of time and dread doing it. When it comes to providing feedback, I've found that women are very good giving and receiving feedback, because we know if we want to get promoted, we need to be on the "right track."

I've noticed that many women who have made it to the top have nothing more to prove. Once they make it to the top, all they really want is for the company to excel, so they think more about their team and the organization in general, rather than themselves. It is not about their egos or how much publicity they have; it is much more about the success of the company, which means thinking about the future of the individuals. In that way, women can be quite inspirational leaders because we tend to genuinely care about the organization, as well as the individual.

Fewer Corporate Scandals

In the McKinsey & Company report titled Women in the Workplace,[21] they found that companies with more women on their board are less likely to be caught up in corporate scandals. Companies that ranked in the bottom quarter in terms of gender diversity on their boards were hit by 24 percent more governance related controversies than average.

---

[21] McKinsey & Co., Women in the Workplace 2018, https://womenintheworkplace. com/Women_in_the_Workplace_2018.pdf

There is unusually strong consensus within academic research that a greater number of women on the board improves performance on corporate and social governance metrics.

A study from researchers at Wake Forest and UNC Wilmington looked at how ethically a company's higher-ups behave when it comes to paying taxes and reporting income based on the gender of the CFO. The research shows that, in general, female CFOs were less prone to riskier tax-avoidance measures that could lead to illegal actions, like tax evasion. It could be due to the argument that women are more ethical when it comes to accurately reporting a company's finances. The paper cites prior research which found that women tend to be more driven by desire for growth and development, while men are generally more driven by the pursuit of money and power—which could lead men to make decisions based strictly on economics, rather than other factors, like a sense of fairness or propriety.[22]

In an article entitled "Boards Without Women Breed Scandal," the Financial Times states, "Public companies with more women on their boards are less likely to be hit by scandals such as bribery, fraud or shareholder battles, according to research from index provider MSCI, which looked at more than 6,500 company boards globally. The research found that boards with gender diversity above and beyond regulatory mandates or market norms had fewer instances of governance-related scandals. There is a clear pattern between having higher than mandated percentages of women on boards and fewer governance-related controversies."[23]

"Ego so often gets in the way of good decision-making in the C-suite. Women exhibit ego differently, and they are good at decision-

---

[22] White, Gillian B, For Less Corporate Fraud, Add Female Executives, The Atlantic, Feb. 2015, https://www.theatlantic.com/business/archive/2015/02/for-less-corporate-fraud-add-female-executives/385618/

[23] Sophia Grene and Chris Newlands, Boards Without Women Breed Scandal, March 8, 2015, Financial Times, https://on.ft.com/2XMr2ge

making with the ego held in check. This is a key advantage in working with boards of directors, partners and customers," says Joan Wrabetz, CTO, Quali.[24]

Because women are somewhat outsiders when it comes to men's circles in an organization, we can offer objectivity and unbiased views. Men will pick their buddies to be on the board. Well, we're *not* buddy buddies with the rest of the board members, so women are the ones who actually can question ideas and be more objective with their viewpoints. When we do lean in and use our voices, it's easier for us to say, "Well, hang on, let's look at this objectively," and "This may not make sense," and "Why are we doing this?"

Improved Revenue

There is a plethora of evidence showing that having more women in senior leadership results in improved profitability for the companies. Given the following statistics, you really have to wonder why companies wouldn't do more to ensure that there are more women at the top.

In "Delivering Through Diversity 2017," McKinsey & Company studied one thousand companies throughout 12 countries. Results showed that companies in the top quartile for gender diversity on executive teams were 21 percent more likely to outperform on profitability and 27 percent more likely to have superior value creation.[25]

The Peterson Institute for International Economics did a working paper in 2016 asking if gender diversity is profitable. The institute studied 22,000 firms globally. The presence of female executives is associated with unusually strong firm performance. When 30 percent of leaders are women, a profitable firm could expect to add more than

---

[24] Replicon, 17 Reasons Women Make Great Leaders, https://www.replicon.com/17-reasons-women-make-great-leaders/amp/

[25] McKinsey & Co., Delivering through Diversity, Jan. 2018, https://www.mckinsey.com/~/media/mckinsey/business%20functions/organization/our%20insights/delivering%20through%20diversity/delivering-through-diversity_full-report.ashx

1 percent to its net margin, compared with an otherwise similar firm with no female leaders. The typical profitable firm in their sample had a net profit margin of 6.4 percent, so a 1 percent point increase represents a 15 percent boost to profitability. Results suggest the real economic payoff is from increasing gender diversity in the C-suite and not on boards.

One study analyzed 1,643 companies that are covered by the MSCI World Index and found that organizations with strong female leadership scored an average 10.1 percent return on equity from the end of 2009 to September 2015, compared with 7.4 percent for companies without women at the most senior levels. MSCI defines strong female leadership as those companies that have three or more women on the board, or a female CEO and at least one other female board member.[26]

Similarly, a study of companies in the United Kingdom, United States, and India by the accountancy firm Grant Thornton[27] found companies perform better when they have at least one female executive on the board.

Lois P. Frankel explains the benefits of female leadership in *See Jane Lead (Frankel, 2009)*:

> The law firm Dickstein Shapiro reports that it had 63 women attorneys out of 213 in 1994, and the per-partner profit was $364,000 annually. Ten years later, when the number of women had grown to 122 out of 363 attorneys, the per-partner profit increased to $815,000. Linda Kornfeld and Robin Cohen, attorneys with Dickstein Shapiro, attribute many reasons they believe women leaders make greater contributions, including:

---

[26] Eling Lee, Linda and Marshall, Ric, et al, Women on Boards, MSCI.com, Nov. 2015 https://www.msci.com/documents/10199/04b6f646-d638-4878-9c61-4eb91748a82b]

[27] Women in Business: The Value of Diversity, GrantThornton, https://www.grantthornton.global/globalassets/wib_value_of_diversity.pdf

- Women executives are more likely to consult with others—experts, employees, and fellow business owners—when developing strategies.

- Women executives have a greater natural tendency to deal comfortably with multitasking.

- Women executives stress relationship building, as well as fact gathering.

- Women executives are more likely to talk through business approaches and incorporate the ideas of others before making final decisions."[28]

Finally, applied research in organizational behavior by Elsevier titled, "Women in high places: When and why promoting women into top positions can harm them individually or as a group (and how to prevent this)" shows a positive correlation between the number of women in leadership positions and customer demand services (e.g., Joy, Carter, Wagner, & Narayanan, 2007). A balanced gender ratio in supervisory or leadership positions helps companies satisfy the needs of its customers and positions them to better serve diverse, often fluctuating, markets.[29]

Better Results For Female Employees

Alana Semuels, author of "When Women Run Companies" (The Atlantic, Dec. 2016)[30] reveals that women tend to improve when under the leadership of other women. This tendency helps women advance.

---

[28] *See Jane Lead*, Ibid.

[29] Ellemer, Naomi, et al, "Women in high places: When and why promoting women into top positions can harm them individually or as a group (and how to prevent this)," *ScienceDirect*, Volume 32, 2012.

[30] Semuels, Alana, When Women Run Companies, What happens to employees under female leadership?, The Atlantic, DEC 27, 2016

It also expands into compensation. One of the reasons for this is that some male bosses may be biased, which can result in men getting compensated more than women, as described previously. In general, female bosses do not think like this. We want to be fair and treat everyone in a transparent, inclusive, and merit-based manner.

In addition, the research also showed another benefit: the more female leaders a firm had, the better they performed. The study suggested that the reason for both of these benefits is that women are better able to read other women and, thus, tend to be better at assigning them to jobs that align with their experience. When women are placed in roles that are a good match for their skills and abilities, those women perform better. For some, that is common sense; however, not everyone can recognize the skills, abilities, and experience that need to be identified to do this well. This study, though, does state that women are more adept at this task than their male peers.

GENDER DIVERSITY OFFERS NEW OPPORTUNITIES AND A COMPETITIVE ADVANTAGE

Women now represent the largest growth opportunity in the world. They will soon represent more than 50 percent of all university students worldwide and by 2028, will control 75 percent of discretionary spending globally. They should, therefore, be equally represented at all levels of companies, especially at the top.

In "Women Matter: Time to accelerate (Ten years of insights into gender diversity)[31], the report concluded some no brainers: (1) closing the global gender gap could boost global GDP (globally women represent 51 percent of the world's working age population but generate only 37 percent of GDP); (2) companies that commit

---

[31] Women Matter—Time to Accelerate, McKinsey and Company, October, 2017, https://www.mckinsey.com/featured-insights/gender-equality/women-matter-ten-years-of-insights-on-gender-diversity/de-de

to diverse leadership are more successful and (3) a better gender mix among the board is linked to higher return on equity, higher valuation, better stock performance, and higher dividend payouts.

Not only that, the benefits of a gender diverse workplace include:

- A company's ability to attract, develop, and retain the talent it needs to compete;

- Improved quality of decision making: diverse and inclusive groups make better quality decisions, often faster and in a more fact-based manner;

- Increased innovation and customer insight;

- Increased employee satisfaction—helps reduce conflict between groups, improving collaboration and loyalty;

- Improved company's global image.

The documented benefits of increased diversity in top management teams – due to an increase of women in high places – indicate that corporate boards – which have to make complex strategic decisions on a daily basis – can perform better when they make use of a range of different skills, knowledge, and experiences (Hoogendoorn, Oosterbeek, & Van Praag, 2011).[32] Qualified people most likely come from different backgrounds as well as genders. It's the combination and consideration of different points of view that makes (gender) diversity a competitive advantage.

The added value of gender diversity in top management teams does not necessarily depend on whether men and women actually approach leadership with different styles. Instead, the quality of the collaboration between different people at work, as well as their success

---

[32] Ellemer, Naomi, et al, Women in high places: When and why promoting women into top positions can harm them individually or as a group (and how to prevent this)," *ScienceDirect*, Volume 32, 2012.

as a team, is enhanced when they explicitly consider the possibility that such differences are present and examine how this might benefit their common goals.

Once again, awareness can affect outcomes.

I think all these factors combine to make the case that women have not only the ability to become great leaders, but also the responsibility to do so. In *See Jane Lead*, Dr. Frankel concurs. She writes that we live in a time ". . . when women's leadership and influence aren't just needed—they're required. More important, I know that women have the capability, strength, courage, and heart to lead communities, businesses, nonprofit organizations, and grassroots groups to places they need to go."[33]

However, in order to have women in leadership roles, companies have to feed their leadership pipeline. And women have to step into the role of leader.

---

[33] *See Jane Lead*, Ibid.

Chapter 5

*Sisterhood is the Solution;
the PMS Project is the Strategy*

The workplace needs sisterhood. When our sisters win through collaboration, we win, too. When women act on behalf of other women, our circle of support will widen, and the number of women in senior positions will grow. Sisterhood means we support each other as we climb the career ladder. We certainly need men to help drive gender equality since they still hold most of the senior positions; but we, as women, can do so much more to help each other. And most of the things we can do are really simple. If we truly want more women at the top in leadership positions across all professions, we must show solidarity. It's time to bring sisterhood into the workplace.

HOW DO WE DO IT?

It starts with awareness and discussion. All the "mean girl" books (*I Can't Believe She Did That* by Nan Moody, *Mean Girls, Meaner Women* by Dr. Erika Holiday and Dr. Joan I. Rosenberg, *Mean Girls at Work* by Katherine Crowley and Kathi Elster) say basically the same thing: it starts with awareness, it starts with talking about it, and it starts by stating what we agree with, what we don't agree with, and what we can do to encourage support for each other. It starts with *us*.

It goes back to that Tina Fey quote in *Mean Girls*: "If you call each other bitches and whores, then it gives the men the right to call you bitches and whores." As Dr. Erika Holiday states in her book, *Mean Girls, Meaner Women*, "Each time a woman devalues another woman, she inevitably devalues herself."[1]

On the flip side, if women call each other "excellent and smart" or "professional and outstanding" or "consistent and confident," I suspect that would give men and women the impetus to call us the same. As a collective of sisters, we can utilize and leverage our network to support each other. Being a great sister means being supportive, stopping the stereotyping, and dropping the double standards.

Support

According to the McKinsey study[2] women are just as ambitious as men, but require a supportive environment in which to succeed. Collective factors (overall environment and corporate culture) are twice as important as individual factors (individual mindset and attitudes) in conditioning women's confidence in their chances of success (as a perception of one's chances of success in their current environment, rather than confidence in one's qualifications).

In simple terms, women need the support of female colleagues who have their backs in order to succeed and thrive in the workplace.

If we support each other more, if we are vocal about helping each other, and if we say positive things about another woman, regardless

---

[1] Holiday, Erika Holiday, Dr. Rosenberg, Joan I., *Mean Girls, Meaner Women: Understanding Why Women Backstab, Betray and Trash-Talk Each Other and How to Heal*, (Orchid Press, 2009)

[2] McKinsey & Co., Women Matter: Time to Accelerate, Oct. 2017, https://www.mckinsey.com/~/media/McKinsey/Featured%20Insights/Women%20matter/Women%20Matter%20Ten%20years%20of%20insights%20on%20the%20importance%20of%20gender%20diversity/Women-Matter-Time-to-accelerate-Ten-years-of-insights-into-gender-diversity.ashx

of what job level she is, it will make a significant difference. Why? Because it goes against the whole, "Oh my gosh, women just cat fight with each other, they're so jealous, they're so (pick your negative and fill in the blank)."

Imagine a meeting where you witness one woman say "Great job" to her female colleague. Picture being able to discuss work-life balance issues with a trusted female leader and ally, one who can offer help or a friendly ear. Visualize a boardroom where instead of only one woman, there are more like five, eight, or ten, and they vocally support their female colleagues at the table. That goes against all the stereotypes we've discussed in previous chapters, and it shows women actually working well together. What a concept!

Showing public support, instead of hiding behind private put-downs, is what we need a lot more of. It's also one of the easiest things we can do to get more women in senior management, as well as more women happy to be at work, period.

Within each company, support doesn't have to be something as formal as a gender equality network. A woman could begin in her workplace with small groups of women who get together and agree to speak positively with and about other women in the office. They just decide—it doesn't have to be formalized. The group members support the women they believe in, rather than gripe about the women they don't, and demonstrate encouragement and praise for jobs well done. A little positive reinforcement goes a long way.

For example, when my girlfriend isn't feeling good about herself, I tell her, "You are amazing, you are the best, you've got this." We have so many insecurities, but we can change that if we support each other emotionally. When I was going through my divorce, I was working at an NGO and didn't get paid much. I knew I needed to find a new job. I was worried, scared, and had zero confidence that I could find a decent, well-paying one. A dear girlfriend said to me, "You've got this. I believe in you. If you were a horse in a race, I would always bet on you, because you're a winner." I've never forgotten that. I love her to this day for saying that to me when I needed it most.

Support can come from anyone. During the time I was going through my divorce, I didn't know how to handle that. It was my sisters, friends, and girlfriends who all came around me, took me out to lunch, and gave me words of encouragement. When I was facing challenges at an investment bank, working a lot of hours, and doubting whether I could handle raising children and the workload, it was my girlfriends who said, "We know you can do it. You're amazing." That kind of encouragement is something your girlfriends can provide.

We need to do this for all our sisters, not just our friends.

Most women who are married and in their thirties, whether with children or not, are at a time in their career when the workload starts getting much more difficult. That's when women need the support system more than ever. I know so many women who just get stressed out, because it's so hard. We don't feel like we are being good mothers, good wives, or good employees. We just want to give up because it is so difficult to juggle everything.

Even if we were to just focus on our job, that in itself is challenging. Trying to climb the career ladder is not easy—it's like walking a minefield every day to make sure you juggle "correctly" between masculine and feminine, without going too much against stereotypes so people will like you. Sisterhood, to me, is about giving each other the support and confidence to help one another. When you're feeling like, "Oh, I want to give up," or "This is too hard," that's when we need to be there for support and a morale boosting exercise.

When I lacked confidence to do something, my husband, girlfriends, or mentors were the ones who would push me forward. When I felt down at work, my friends would lift me up. We get so busy at work that sometimes we don't make time for friends, family, colleagues, mentors, etc. That is a big mistake. When we are down, they are the ones who will encourage us – they are our support network. We cannot underestimate how important they are.

Support From Working Moms

As a working mom, I never understood the "soccer moms"—those moms who could stay at school or at after-school activities all day to help out. They never liked me, either, since I was working, instead of at home taking care of my kids. We were judging each other without even knowing each other. But I realized they could be my allies when I was at work.

I befriended one of these moms when my son was about 10 years old. "It's really hard for me to know what's going on in school because I don't have any time to spend there," I said. "It's very admirable of you to spend time there so that you know what's going on with your children. I feel bad that I can't do the same." Then we became friends, and she became my eyes and ears at the school.

One time she called me and said, "Okay, Jaclyn, I want to talk to you about your son, Greg. Today, I noticed that he ate lunch by himself. You might want to talk to him about it. Maybe something's wrong." When I got home, I said to Greg, "What's going on? Why were you eating lunch by yourself?" I have to say he was really surprised.

He said, "How did you know that?" I replied with a grin, "I'm a mother; I know everything." He explained how he got into an argument with one of his friends. That really helped me a lot when my children were young, to have friends like that. You can learn a lot from stay-at-home moms.

I tell women who are working and who have children, "You know what? Be friends with the women who hang out in the schools. Don't think of them as being so different from you that you have nothing you can relate to." I say, "They can be really great allies." Those kinds of things that you learn are some of the tips you can pass on to your female colleagues. Also, share tips on how to achieve work-life balance.

It's a constant struggle, so let's share notes on what works and what doesn't. For example, I tell working moms they shouldn't stress about not spending enough time with the kids because it's about the quality of the time, not the quantity of the time.

Another example: I discovered that, often, mothers come home, they're tired, and they'll ask, "How was your day? How was school?" Yawn. Their child would usually say, "Fine, it's fine." Instead, I started by telling them how my day was and spinning it into a story that was fun. I would say things like, "Oh, I had a really tough day today with this hone guy who was giving me a hard time." They would remember the story and would say to me the next day, "Oh, Mom, how did you deal with that issue? How did it go?" We would have very interactive dialogue, and they would speak to me a lot more. I think that helped in terms of my relationship with my sons because they're very, very close to me. They're very open with me. I think it's about sharing, and not just about "how was your day?".

SUPPORT FROM OUR GIRLFRIENDS

Every year, I try to go away with some of my friends on a "girls' trip. It's so important to keep your friendships. Women will say, "I'm so busy at work, I just don't have time." I tell them this is one area you have to continue working on. I've always done that. When I go to New York or Singapore, for example, I make sure to reach out to my girlfriends in advance and say, "I'm going to be there these days and those days. Let's make sure we meet for dinner."

Anywhere I go, if have friends there, I make it a point to meet them and spend time with them. At Hong Kong University, I volunteer my time at what's called the CEO Global. It is an NGO that goes to the best universities to educate students on the soft skills, such as core values of leadership, including integrity, communication, and relationships. They discuss all different aspects of being a good leader.

One of the games we play is a fake auction game. We tell them, "Okay, pretend you have one million dollars, and we're going to auction off all of these different things. You guys raise your hand and bid, but once you use up your money, that's it." There were various things on that auction list, including, for example, being the CEO of a company, having free education for life, having an island of your own, or having a huge house wherever you wanted.

But interestingly, the one that's always most popular and always the one that students tend to "buy" is having three best friends who they can talk to and trust for life. I will ask the students, "Why would you do that, spend all of your money on that? That's something you can easily create. You don't have to spend your money."

They said, "No, it's not easy to create. I cannot even imagine having great friends that I can trust for the rest of my life because we're all so busy doing our own thing." I find it astonishing, and it's men and women alike who go for that. To me, it's a reminder to work at our relationships and treat them with value and respect; otherwise, they won't last, and it's not something that can be bought. I encouraged those students to make sure to keep up the friendships they made throughout childhood, university, and the workplace. Make the time. That's so crucial, because when you're down, they're the ones who are going to be there for you.

STOP THE STEREOTYPING AND THE DOUBLE STANDARDS

As we've illustrated many times, the negative stereotyping of successful women that we help perpetuate holds other women back. Don't allow people to describe a successful senior woman as "dragon lady" or "bitchy" or "unfriendly." This helps nothing and no one, and it brings us all down in the process.

We need to stop allowing and joining in on the stereotypes. If a woman is saying something catty about another woman, we shouldn't engage in that. In fact, if we know that's not true, we should say that's not true.

Let's be more supportive and understand these stereotypes better and say, "Okay, well let's not apply these stereotypes so much. Let's not expect that female boss to be fantastic all the time." Like I've said, because there are fewer female role models, there's a lot of pressure on that female to do a great job than there would be on a male, because women are likely to say, "I never want a female boss." As a female leader, there is so much pressure to be great, but we have our insecurities, too. It's this double standard that other women put on female leaders that makes it so difficult. Sisters, drop the double standards.

At the same time, we have to juggle work, and we have to deal with all the corporate politics. We don't have 100 percent of our time to be able to be encouraging all the time, to be a nurturer all the time, and it's hard. It's hard to juggle all of the expectations. As mentioned in the last chapter, there are a lot of studies that show there's always higher expectations on women than men.

Let's put an end to the stereotyping. If you hear women being catty about another woman, let's stop them and offer some positive comments instead. If someone says a manager is a bitch, then say, "No, she is a strong woman." If someone says a director is aggressive, say, "No, she just knows what she wants." If someone says she's bossy, then say, "No, she is a leader."

We need to praise those who have a flair for self-promotion and understand the political savvy it takes to get to the top, rather than being our fiercest critics.

THE BENEFITS OF SISTERHOOD

If we bring sisterhood in the workplace, there's no doubt that we will reduce the pay gap, because the department heads who are women are more likely to make sure there is no gap.

More women will stay in the workplace because they will have a support network. So many women drop out before they even get there. This is especially important for women in mid-level positions, because that's when it becomes really hard.

From what I've noticed, a lot of women don't apply for a promotion or a certain job because unless they can tick off 100 percent of the requirements, they don't apply. Men only feel the need to tick off 50 percent to apply for a job they want. That can be attributed to confidence, but if you have a support system that says, "So what if you don't meet all of the requirements! Once they meet you, they'll see how amazing you are, and you're smart enough that you'll be able to learn whatever you need to do." Sisterhood builds confidence.

START A MOVEMENT. EMBRACE THE PMS PROJECT.

I came up with this idea after learning about those who say they'd never support a woman president due to PMS. I thought, *Why not turn PMS to a positive?* Since it's only women supposedly who experience it, I decided to change the PMS acronym into something more positive that applies to women.

It's important to me because I think it all goes hand in hand with helping one another so there are more women at the top. This PMS Project is about what women can do for each other; and every one of us should think like that—each of us should feel like we own part of this problem.

Sisterhood is the umbrella and philosophy that permeates PMS. As women go up the ladder, they progress through PMS:

P is for Promoter and can start at any level in a woman's career, from an assistant up to CEO, and can come from anyone . . . including yourself.

M is for Mentor. As women become more knowledgeable and move up the ladder, they become mentors. Mentors talk with you.

S is for Sponsor. As these mentors become even more senior with more influence, they become a sponsor. Sponsors talk about you.

Let's take a closer look at each one.

Promoter

There are many ways to promote our sisters in the workplace. An example we already discussed is by showing vocal support for our female colleagues. When we see other women doing a great job, regardless of her position, we should say so. Remember, it's an easy thing to do that is not only subtle, but effective.

It's definitely harder for women to speak about what we've done. When working with my team, I will always say, "We, we, we, we" . . . as in my group, as in my team. I want to make it collective.

We can help other women become more visible. For example, I've asked my CEO to have lunch with the women in my team. These are the types of things that can really help promote each other's visibility. When I see some of the women not sitting at the table in a large meeting, I'll say, "Come take a seat next to me," in order to encourage them to join and be seen. There are many things we can do to build each other's confidence. It gives leaders the opportunity to see women they may not have noticed before, who are smart, capable, and potential leaders.

A Lean In/McKinsey & Company survey in 2016[3] of 132 companies and 34,000 employees found that women who negotiated for promotions were 30 percent more likely than men to be labeled intimidating, bossy, or too aggressive than men who do the same thing. If a smart, capable woman is gunning for the COO or CEO role overtly, studies have shown that she is less likely to get the role because others would view her as too aggressive.

So rather than having her ask for herself, why don't we do it for her? Why don't we become her promoter? As I mentioned, in *Lean In*, Sheryl used the example of the four Merrill Lynch female bankers who decided to promote each other, and they all ended up moving up. So

---

[3] Women Matter 2016, Reinventing the Workplace to Unlock the Potential of Gender Diversity, McKinsey & Company

as promoters, let's celebrate accomplishments for each other. We are often penalized for self-promotion, so instead of (or in addition to) self-promote, let's group promote.

In meetings, performance reviews, and everyday conversations, call out women for their achievements. When women celebrate one another's accomplishments, we're all lifted up.

GIVE PRAISE AND BUILD CONNECTIONS

According to the KPMG Women's Leadership Study, more than half of working women indicate that receiving praise from colleagues, leaders, and mentors most influences their perceptions of themselves in the workplace, versus traditional rewards of raises and promotions.[4] (Women leaders know this, so we tend to give feedback more often.)

Here are some additional ways to promote your sister in a way that works best for her:

- Provide opportunities for women to be visible in front of the "right" people.

- Identify and develop those high-performing women who aspire to lead.

- Provide the kind of individual feedback that reinforces and builds confidence and high performance.

- Build effective networks with the express goal of generating opportunities for women's promotion and leadership growth.

- Actively give qualified women leadership opportunities.

- Put in place challenging and aspirational career paths for women at work.

---

[4] KPMG's Women's Leadership Study, https://home.kpmg/content/dam/kpmg/ph/pdf/ThoughtLeadershipPublications/KPMGWomensLeadershipStudy.pdf

Mentor

I think all women ideally should have a mentor. A mentor is someone who can help you navigate your career and provide guidance. The mentee drives the relationship. Mentoring can start at any level, as long as there is someone below you! There is always someone who's younger and less experienced that may need help—for example, college students. I mentor many college students from Hong Kong University, and it's because they really don't know what they want to do sometimes. They do need a lot of guidance.

To me, mentoring is like passing the baton. Once you have made it, pass the baton to a woman below you who needs guidance. Like the cover of this book, I also envision it as women who are on the corporate ladder: there's a woman on top, and she has her hand reaching down to pull the person up the ladder. I'm giving my hand to you, just grab it, and let's climb up together.

Women need female mentors. KPMG found that 82 percent of women believe that access to and networking with female leaders would help advance her career.[5] According to the same study, 67 percent of women reported that they would learn the most important lessons about leadership from other women. If each of us took the time to mentor, we could leave a legacy of amazing, great female leaders. Remember how hard it was for you, so help them go through it. When you mentor someone you also get so much *out* of it, because it helps you become a better leader, a better listener, and a better person.

In Chapter 7, we'll discuss in greater detail the mentorship process and how to leverage relationships in the workplace.

---

[5] Ibid.

Sponsor

Sponsorship is about identifying junior women who you think have potential and making an effort to sponsor them. It also means senior women asking senior men to sponsor junior women. And remember, by being a part of the sisterhood by supporting, promoting, and mentoring the women around you, the result will be more women at the top who can be sponsors.

A sponsor is a senior leader who uses strong influence to help you obtain high-visibility, promotions, etc. The sponsor drives the relationship. He or she is your advocate, including behind closed doors. They believe in your potential and act as your advocate to make sure you are considered for key roles.

Here are some steps you can take to become a sponsor:

- Identify a female candidate you have worked with or observed at work who has made a strong, positive impression on you.

- Connect with her and explain you want to help her and why.

- Ask about her career aspirations and long-term goals.

Sheryl Sandberg, the COO of Facebook, admits that her rise to the top was due in large part to Larry Summers, who was her sponsor. We'll discuss more about sponsorship in the chapter 7.

We Can Do it!

We are women, we are incredible, and once we put our mind on a task, we get it done, we are doers. We can make the workplace a collaborative and cooperative culture that benefits every woman. If we want more women at the top, we need to show solidarity and encourage each other. It is time to take an honest look at how we treat one another in the workplace and strive for greater professionalism and support.

Rather than pick on the flaws and be each other's fiercest critics, we need to acknowledge those who have succeeded. We need to praise those who have a flair for self-promotion and understand the political savvy it takes to get to the top. If we hear women being catty about another woman, stop them, point it out, and replace those comments with positive ones. Let's be Sisters, and Promoters, Mentors, and Sponsors.

Chapter 6

How to Succeed as a Female Boss

In addition to all the qualities that people need to be a successful boss, I have found that women are generally happier and stay with an employer longer if (1) her job fits well with the other areas of her life, (2) she enjoys the work, (3) her job gives her the opportunity to make a difference, and (4) she feels connected to the organization. According to "What Women Want in the Workplace,"[1] those are the top four out of ten. In other words, women want to work for a company that has a good sense of values (a culture of professionalism and collaboration across departments); provides an opportunity to learn, grow, and take on new assignments or roles; treats people with fairness and respect; offers opportunities that make best use of that employee's skills; and that enables them to make a meaningful, relevant contribution to the company.[2]

There are many strategies a woman can use to increase her chances of not only having what she wants in the workplace, but also of becoming a woman at the top.

---

[1] Lean In, Women in the Workplace, Women are Doing Their Part; Now Companies Need to do Their Part, Too, https://womenintheworkplace.com/Women_in_the_Workplace_2017.pdf

[2] What do Women Want from Work, Center for Creative Leadership, Feb. 2019, https://www.ccl.org/blog/what-women-want-work/

UNDERSTAND THE BUSINESS AND KNOW THE NUMBERS

For women to succeed, you have to understand the strategy of the company you work for. People forget the importance of business, strategic, and financial acumen. Senior management thinks of these as "givens," but many women forget that these are required, basic skills.

A lot of women I've known don't realize how important that is. It doesn't matter if you are in the revenue generating part of the business, such as sales, or back office, such as operations. In order to make it to the top, we have to understand the strategy of the company and understand its financials.

In her TED Talk, "The Career Advice You Probably Didn't Get," Susan Colantuono (on an executive panel on the topic of "What do you look for in high-potential employees?") posed a key question to an audience. In addition to looking for people who are smart, hardworking, committed, and trustworthy, Susan proposed: "What about people who are able to scan the external environment, identify risks and opportunities, make strategy or make strategic recommendations? And what about people who are able to look at the financials of your business, understand the story that the financials tell, and either take appropriate action or make appropriate recommendations?"

She said that a man replied, "That's a given."

She then turned to the audience of 150 women and asked, "How many of you have ever been told that the door-opener for career advancement is your business, strategic and financial acumen, and that all the other important stuff is what differentiates you in the talent pool?" Three women raised their hand. Her point was that the most important skill—business, strategic and financial acumen—is missing in the advice given to women. This is not because women are incapable of achieving this skill, but rather they aren't told that is a skill that they need to acquire.

At the end of the day, you can tell a lot about a company by just looking at the numbers. Men seem better able to do that, and they seem better able to see things in broader pictures, not just in their particular area—may be it is because they already know that in order to succeed they need to do these things because they are "givens." I think women need to do more of that in order to advance into leadership. We can do it, but we're so focused on doing well in our own department that we forget that, if we want to make it to the top, we have to be able to look at the company from a strategic and financial perspective, like the owner of the company would. If we don't, management will think we're only good in our one area, and nothing more.

PRACTICE FAIRNESS

I always try to be fair to both men and women. This can be with respect to pay, flexi-hours or promotions. For example, one woman on my team wanted to take almost a whole day off to go to her son's school show. Now, if anybody else wanted to take time off, they would just take it as a leave, or half a leave, according to corporate policy. She reported to a man, and he told me, "Well, I have to approve this. She doesn't want to take it as a day leave, but she'll just go." I said to him, "Wait, hang on. You have to be fair, because men or women who don't have children would have to take that time off as a leave." I said, "I don't mind if she goes for a few hours, and then comes to work late, or she makes it up during lunchtime or whatever works for her, but you have to always think about being fair to people who have kids and those who don't."

I think women are better at judging what's fair. I think women look at all situations and apply equal standards, whereas men may approve things because the person asking is his buddy or it makes them look good in front of others, but that doesn't equate to being a good leader.

BE A TRANSFORMATIONAL LEADER—
DEVELOP YOUR TEAM

I am a big fan of constant learning and personal development. I think a leader should try to support and develop their team, so they can succeed. My team may not love that I do this, but I usually give them tasks that are challenging and outside their comfort zone. I do it because I know that if they want to be a leader one day, they are going to have to do it. I try to groom everyone for the next level, and it doesn't matter to me if it's a man or a woman. Most of the female leaders do the same.

According to Vanessa Van Edwards, author of *Huffpost's* "Battle of the Sexes: Male vs. Female Leadership," a female leader should "seek to be a role model who inspires their subordinates; invest a lot of time in coaching their team members and care about their personal development; and emphasize teamwork and authentic communication as a key to success. Look for ways to inspire your team members to be more motivated in accomplishing your goals."[3]

Most organizations are still far too opaque in their processes, which means all involved, not only women, are left unsure exactly what they have to do to succeed. Organizations need to be clear about what is required to progress, and about the exact impact taking time out to have a family or going on flextime for whatever reason will have on careers. These should not be closed-door conversations that lead everyone to think that someone else is getting a better deal.

---

[3] Van Edwards, Vanessa, "Battle of the Sexes: Male vs. Female Leadership," *Huffington Post, July, 2017,* https://www.huffingtonpost.com/entry/battle-of-the-sexes-male-vs-female-leadership_us_59647ddbe4b09be68c00551a

SHARE WITH THE TEAM—OVER COMMUNICATE

A *Science of People* article, entitled "Women in Leadership: 6 Strategies for Female Managers," stresses the importance of communication:

> As we learned, female bosses are already naturally inclined to verbally communicate. This is one of the keys to success. When your team feels comfortable being transparent with you, you're less likely to have to deal with major problems because they feel safe coming to you for help the moment issues start to arise.
>
> Remind your team why their work matters. Find something that makes each and every one of your team member's work meaningful. Your goal should be to make them feel like they are doing something greater than working for a paycheck. As women, we have a tremendous opportunity to be incredible bosses and managers. All we have to do is leverage our natural, positive female strengths and put them into action.[4]

Part of the need to share with your team is because it instills trust from the team. Successful women leaders are trustworthy. When you establish a climate of trust, your team commits to goals, is willing to work better as a team, and ideas are shared more freely. More importantly, employees are more comfortable with change and are more willing to embrace a new vision.

OFFER SUPPORT FOR WORK-LIFE BALANCE ISSUES

As we've discussed and we all know from personal experience, women deal with more child care, household operation, family obligations, and physical considerations than the average man. If a woman is having difficulties with her child or difficulties with her marriage, she is much more likely than a man to come and talk to me about those problems. I always try to help them in terms of how to deal with work-life balance

---

[4] Women in Leadership: 6 Strategies for Female Managers, Science of People, https://www.scienceofpeople.com/women-in-leadership/

issues. I would refer them to pediatricians I know, or girlfriends who may be in the same situation and able to help. Women need each other's support. We've been through what they've been through. We can help lead and support each other during times of crisis or upset. To me, that's part of being a good leader.

BE A GREAT ROLE MODEL

You have to earn their respect. Remember (as if we could forget), everyone's watching you, and women are emulating you. It's incumbent upon women leaders to set good examples. Women need role models that we want to emulate and aspire to ... and be inspired by.

Oftentimes, there are many smart, capable women who drop out of the corporate environment. Something happens where they're working on a deal, and it's extremely exhausting, and they think, *Okay, I don't want to do this anymore, and I give up.* To me, if women had more examples of women who have made it and somehow have been able to juggle everything, it inspires them to think instead, *You know what, I can do it, too.*

If you have more women at the top, more women can be sponsors and help other women reach the top. Another benefit of having more women who are at the top—let's say 30 to 40 percent more women— is that with the higher the numbers, a woman will be less compelled toward unhealthy competition, because she'll see that at least one-third of us are going to make it.

I used to be the only female executive committee member at my company. I constantly felt that I had to set the right example, because if I didn't, I would be making it easier to label women in general about my individual leadership abilities. As a female leader who wants women to want to work with female leaders, I feel compelled to set the right examples all the time so people won't generalize me. It is difficult because you feel that you are constantly being watched, assessed and judged. Remember, men are continually applauded for being ambitious, powerful, and successful, but women who display these same traits often pay a social penalty.

I've never had a direct female boss, but I have worked with women who were very successful in the organization. I must admit, however, I've seen some really bad examples of women as leaders. In one of the companies I worked for, there were two very senior women who disliked each other, and everyone knew they didn't like each other because they fought openly with each other all the time. Colleagues would joke about it and say things like, "Look at them. They can't do anything but cat fight."

In another example, I asked a very senior woman who, again, I didn't work for directly, why she didn't pass some of her clients to someone else. She'd say things like, "Oh, because none of the girls are pretty enough to cover my accounts." She gave a lunch presentation once and told the women that they always have to wear makeup and look good and pretty; otherwise, they won't be able to have accounts. This was a horrible example for other women. We all laughed and joked about it, but we were also thinking, *How can we have a woman like that in the company?*

Hopefully these types of female leaders are relics of the past. I believe the next level of women, both my peers and below, realize this and, as a result, we try harder to be better bosses and set good examples. I definitely see more and more successful women who understand the difficulties and plight of younger women because they've lived them. I see women coming up the ladder who I think would make phenomenal examples of female bosses.

HAVE STRENGTH AND GRIT

Success requires strength, both emotionally and physically. In particular, women need to be strong enough to stay in the game. They also have to develop a thick skin, one that will enable them to overcome criticisms, untoward remarks, and stereotypes. They have to be confident enough to take risks when they are necessary and have the perseverance and courage to speak up and never give up. There will be challenges, even setbacks, but a strong sense of self-belief will not only benefit women in their career goals, but it will also inspire other women to develop and exhibit the same strengths.

In order to overcome the challenges that will come our way, women need to develop grit—a stay-with-it attitude that helps them overcome adversity and the resulting stress and obstacles that will present themselves. Unfortunately, too many women lack that grit and become frustrated before they achieve their goals. For many, proving that they had the passion and wherewithal to persevere would have provided the outcome they were seeking.

By keeping an eye trained on their long term goals, women can overcome the day-to-day obstacles and challenges that will come their way. Yes, women do have challenges and obstacles that men do not have. For example, a pregnancy might be a celebratory event for a male; however, women may worry that such a life-changing event will put a damper on her career aspirations. This is why it is so important that women remain determined and confident; they have to "prove" that their family and home responsibilities do not make them less qualified or less dedicated.

LEAD WITH YOUR WITS, INFLUENCE, AND MOTIVATIONAL ABILITIES

According to Dr. Frankel in *See Jane Lead*, "Women have traditionally had to lead through their wits, influence, and motivational abilities." They don't have the luxury of power through intimidation. Just try it with a teenager and see how well it works!

I believe we live in a time when women's leadership and influence aren't just needed—they're required. More importantly, I *know* that women have the capability, strength, courage, and heart to lead communities, businesses, nonprofit organizations, and grassroots groups to places they need to go.

Women say that a charismatic, well-adjusted woman at the top goes a long way toward creating a healthy office atmosphere. When powerful and highly visible women are seen helping other women by becoming members of boards or committees, by pushing for women-friendly corporate policies, by mentoring young women, or by simply honoring their word, they set a standard for everyone else.

REIGN IN YOUR EMOTIONS WHEN NEEDED

According to Anne Kreamer, author of *It's Always Personal: Navigating Emotion in the New Workplace,* there's really only one consistently successful way to quell your emotions at work. The good news is that it's an easy one: just get up.

"Say you're in a meeting and you're having a confrontation with somebody who isn't understanding you, and you're about ready to blow up, or you feel tears coming on: go get a drink of water," says Kreamer. Importantly, it's less about water than the moving. "The physical movement begins to reset your parasympathetic nerve system, and put you in a different mind-set and allows you to gather yourself so you can go back in and try to tackle the conversation with a fresh perspective."[5]

At times men can be overly-emotional as well, but as women we must remember to not allow our emotions to get the better of us in the office environment. When you feel frustrated and upset or feel your eyes well up with tears, find a quiet place and call your friends, mentors or sisters for moral support. This is when sisterhood plays a crucial role.

---

[5] Heaney, Katie, The Single Easiest Way to Control Your Emotions at Work, The Cut, June 2018, https://www.thecut.com/2018/06/how-to-control-your-emotions-at-work.html

Chapter 7

Leveraging Relationships to Climb the Ladder

Throughout my career, I hoped I'd find some great female role models to help me, but I wasn't able to—either because there weren't any, or the ones I knew weren't people I wanted to emulate. However, I've been fortunate to have two male mentors throughout my career and have known them for more than 20 years. They've been there during my good times and bad times. They've been my confidante when I needed advice. I'm grateful that I've had such wonderful mentors. This is why it is so surprising to me when I hear from other women that they don't have mentors. They are missing out on an important element of their personal growth and career development.

Women are missing the critical relationships they need to change the course of their careers. The reasons are many, and we've discussed some of them in previous chapters, but among the most pervasive are:

- The leadership pipeline is dominated by males.

- Women's networks are not as fully available or developed among influencers where they work.

- Women often are not part of the networks available to men.

- women resist the idea that "who you know" is helpful in career advancement.

- Seventy-seven percent of surveyed women believed that hard work and long hours, rather than connections, were sufficient for advancement (Harvard Business Review, 2011).

- Men spend 70 percent of their time building relationships "upward," and women do the opposite (Tannen).

- Men are 46 percent more likely to have an active sponsor (Hewlett, 2013)

- Studies show that eight out of ten working women do not even feel confident enough to ask for a mentor and nine out of ten do not feel confident asking for a sponsor.[1]

Now that we know how sisterhood in the workplace could impact these numbers and that the PMS project is the strategy to increase mentorship and sponsorship of women, let's examine both in greater detail.

WHAT'S THE DIFFERENCE BETWEEN A MENTOR AND A SPONSOR?

The biggest difference is a simple one, and Heather Foust-Cummings, a vice president with Catalyst Research Center for Equity in Business Leadership, explained it this way: "A mentor will talk with you, but a sponsor will talk *about* you."[2]

My mentors have helped me tremendously throughout my career. They started out as my bosses, and as I moved to another company, they continued to be my "mentor." Since they know the way I work and my personality, they helped guide me when I had concerns about

---

[1] KPMG's Women's Leadership Study, https://home.kpmg/content/dam/kpmg/ph/pdf/ThoughtLeadershipPublications/KPMGWomensLeadershipStudy.pdf

[2] https://www.forbes.com/sites/shelleyzalis/2018/03/29/a-moment-of-mentorship-can-lead-to-a-lifetime-of-impact/#4b972e1579d2

my career path. They've also been my emotional supporters when I needed them. I cannot stress how important mentors can be because they are the ones you will be able to bounce ideas with, complain to about a particular situation, or ask for sage career and personal advice when needed. When I left The Nature Conservancy and was looking for a new job, my mentor used his influence to call several companies, asking them if they were looking for a lawyer—and if so, he said that they should hire me. He helped me get my initial interview with Morgan Stanley. He was able to vouch for me since I'd worked for him before.

A mentor can also be someone from outside the organization where you work. A mentor could be anyone you admire, respect, and feel you can build a relationship with. She (or he) doesn't even have to be in your field. I have plenty of mentees who do things quite different from law or banking. A mentor is a trusted person with whom you can speak safely about issues impacting your life—whether personal or workplace. Cate Huston puts it this way: "Mentors give you perspective, while sponsors give you opportunities."[3] Put one more way, "Mentors help you 'skill up,' whereas sponsors help you *move* up."[4]

A sponsor is ideally someone within the organization where you work and someone who has influence. A sponsor is someone who is more senior than you and not only recognizes the great job you're doing, but is also willing to speak on your behalf. They are very supportive of your career and will speak highly of you in front of other people. When an opening comes up and they think you are ready for it, they'll put your name forward. They'll talk to you and encourage you to apply.

---

[3] https://www.forbes.com/sites/shelleyzalis/2018/03/29/a-moment-of-mentorship-can-lead-to-a-lifetime-of-impact

[4] Miller, Jo, The People Who can Open More Career Doors than You Ever Thought Possible, The Muse, https://www.themuse.com/advice/the-people-who-can-open-more-career-doors-than-you-ever-thought-possible

A sponsor can be influential within your organization and also outside the organization. A sponsor is someone who worked with you before; therefore, they've seen your work style, the quality of the work you've produced, and your work ethics.

I think the concept of sponsorship has only come along recently. Sponsorship has always been there, but no one really labeled it as something that could be different to mentorship until fairly recently. Interestingly, the studies show that men tend to naturally have more sponsors than women because their mentors tend to become their sponsors; whereas, with women, that progression is not a "norm."

As Jo Miller writes in her article for TheMuse.com, "Having the support of a sponsor is like having a safety net, allowing you to confidently take risks like asking for a stretch assignment or a promotion. They provide a protective bubble and can shield you from organizational change like reorganizations or layoffs. And they bring your name up in those high-level talent development discussions that take place behind closed doors. If your career is moving forward, chances are there's a sponsor behind the scenes, pulling strings on your behalf."[5]

Why Are Both Necessary For Career Advancement For Women?

It definitely helps if you have both. People often ask me, whether at work or at events where I'm presenting, "How do I get a sponsor?" The thing is, it's so much easier to start by getting a mentor. It doesn't require that you ask permission or say, "Oh, will you be my mentor?" It's just reaching out to someone you admire, having coffee with that person, and building a relationship with them.

Mentorship helps because, as the KPMG studies show, women thrive with encouragement, a role model, and someone they can trust

---

[5] Ibid.

and speak to. Throughout my career, there have been times when someone would yell at me and I'd get very upset. I'd close the door and start crying to get it out of my system. I would call my mentor and say, "Yeah, this happened," and they would say, "Don't worry about it. Chill and don't let it get to you."

In the book, *The Confidence Code: The Science and Art of Self-Assurance—What Women Should Know* (Harper Business, 2018), authors Katty Kay and Claire Shipman write that, for the most part, if something goes wrong for a male employee, he shrugs it off. "'I don't dwell on stuff; when it's done, it's done.' We heard the same attitude from most of the men we talked with. Even when they aren't natural performers, they just move through their challenges with less baggage."[6] I've noticed this difference between men and women in my own career. If you say something really negative to a woman, it really gets to her head, and it really affects the woman a lot. This is an area where a mentor can be of immense help.

Having a mentor and being able to "bounce things off of them" helps women be less reactive and emotional about setbacks. Again, just having somebody looking at a situation from a neutral position and being able to say, "It's okay, just brush it off," is a huge catalyst to confidence for women. Mentors will tell you that the difficulty you face is an area you can work on, especially now that you know about it. Mentors say, "Do better and better. Don't worry about it. Keep taking action and move forward." That's what a mentor can do, because mentors want to be supportive.

On the other hand, having a sponsor can make rising through the ranks of your organization a lot easier for you. When they could speak on your behalf if you're not there, without a doubt it's easier for you to get ahead. I definitely believe that. I've been an advocate several times for women who I noticed were doing a great job; I'll try to

---

[6] *The Confidence Code,* Ibid

somehow find a way to get that woman promoted (sometimes even without their knowledge).

However, finding and getting a sponsor is a little trickier. First, the sponsor has to *see or at least hear* that you are doing a great job. The sponsor has to see that you're worthy of advocating. It's not like you can find somebody and ask, "Will you be my sponsor?" That doesn't really work. A sponsor is an influencer and usually someone senior in your company or even a non-executive board member.

You could start with a coffee or dialogue and explain what you've accomplished. For the women who I've sponsored, many weren't even in my department, but I've seen what they'd accomplished and that they were doing a great job. Usually, we would develop a relationship because they would proactively reach out to me by coming into my office and talking to me about what they were working on. They would often have conversations with me about some of the things that they would like to see changed in the organization. (In other words, they *acted* on their own behalf.) Even though they didn't work directly for me, I could see that they were really good at what they did, and that's how I naturally became a sponsor or advocate for them.

As Jo Miller writes, "If you want to advance your career, having a mentor isn't enough anymore. Don't get me wrong—mentors are wonderful. They help you gain critical skills, navigate you through challenges at work, and offer a sounding board when you're at a crossroads in your career. But if you aspire to climb higher in this modern and competitive climate, you'll need a sponsor as well."[7]

One reason so few women hold the really top business positions is that they are rich in mentors, but sorely lacking in sponsors, according to a report at HBR.org ("Women are Over-Mentored But Under-Sponsored").

---

[7] Miller, Jo, The People Who can Open More Career Doors than You Ever Thought Possible, The Muse, https://www.themuse.com/advice/the-people-who-can-open-more-career-doors-than-you-ever-thought-possible

Men's mentors are actually more senior, more influential, and have access to a wider network than women's mentors. In other words, men's mentors are often really sponsors. Men have predominantly male networks, and women have largely female or mixed networks, according to another hbr. org report, from 2019. Since men are more likely to hold senior positions, women may be at a disadvantage when it comes to accessing high-level mentorship and sponsorship. But when women do have sponsors, they are just as likely as men to be promoted.

MENTORSHIP: IT MATTERS

Mentoring relationships between women can be tremendously influential and rewarding. In a 2001 study of mentoring women lawyers[8] sociologist Jean Wallace found female role models provided more emotional and social support, infusing their mentees with greater career satisfaction and job commitment and less work-family conflict. The KPMG study[9] also found that receiving encouragement from role models can help women bridge the confidence gap.

Mentoring is also useful to the mentor because the best way to grow and evolve is to learn from people who are different from you—whether in specialty, department, title, or background. As Shelly Zalis writes for Forbes.com, "The best advice you can get in life often comes from people and places you would not expect. Sure, it's more comfortable to stick to who and what you know. However, stretching yourself by connecting with people who have a different background, perspective, or mindset will enable you to better understand others' viewpoints."[10]

---

[8] Wallace, Jean, The Benefits of Monitoring for Female Lawyers, Science Direct, June, 2001, https://www.sciencedirect.com/science/article/abs/pii/S0001879100917664

[9] KPMG Women's Leadership Study, Ibid.

[10] Zalis, Shelley, Why Mentorship Doesn't Have to be Formal, *Forbes,* March 2018, https://www.forbes.com/sites/shelleyzalis/2018/03/29/a-moment-of-mentorship-can-lead-to-a-lifetime-of-impact/#4b972e1579d2

Pay It Forward

Women say that a charismatic, well-adjusted woman at the top goes a long way toward creating a healthy office atmosphere. When powerful and highly visible women are seen helping other women by becoming members of boards or committees, by pushing for women-friendly corporate policies, by mentoring young women, or by simply honoring their word, they set a standard for everyone else.

Women need to show the way for junior women. I started mentoring when I was a vice president at Morgan Stanley. I didn't wait until I was a Managing Director or even an Executive Director.

Now that you've been able to advance your career because of your hard work, support from others, and taking the necessary steps and sacrifices to get there, pay it forward by investing in a woman who needs your support. If you're early in your career, find a woman who's coming up behind you, like a university student who's interested in your field. It doesn't have to be through a formal mentorship program. You can just do it on your own. It can simply be reaching out to them for coffee or lunch. I have a mentee who recently was promoted. I said to her, "You are now the level where you can definitely be a mentor." She said, "No, no, no, I'm not senior enough. I'm not ready." I told her that there will always be people more junior or less experienced and she needs to pay it forward. If you're an analyst, you can mentor a college student. If you're an executive assistant, you can mentor an assistant.

You can mentor at any time in your career. So, I don't think waiting until being so-called "senior enough" is valid. All you need to do is make it authentic. It doesn't matter what level you're at. If there are women who are more junior to you, start mentoring.

How It Works

While 7 in 10 working women (70 percent) feel a personal obligation to help more women advance in the workplace, only one-third (33 percent) have learned to leverage and support other female employees. Unfortunately, 8 in 10 working women (79 percent) do not even feel confident enough to ask for a mentor and 9 in 10 (92 percent) do not feel confident asking for a sponsor.

So, you can take the lead on someone's behalf who is junior to you. It's one more element of embracing sisterhood. If you see someone junior to you who is struggling, reach out to her. Once the initial contact is made, it can be the mentee who drives the relationship forward, so that a bond forms. The mentees need to be flexible in setting a time and date when meeting a potential mentor and should make the effort to reach out on a regular basis. Once a relationship starts to form, at that point both will make an effort to reach out to each other.

A mentor/mentee relationship is based on a deeper, more meaningful connection with someone you trust. It takes time and effort to form this meaningful relationship. I still reach out to my mentors, one of whom is now retired. But we will have lunch and catch up, and now the discussions are about retiring and/or the next "phase" in our lives. My mentors know me and my work style, so I trust their views.

A "cheat sheet" is a great tool to create for those you choose to mentor. You have experiences as a working single mom, or a wife in a marriage balancing career demands with your husband, or how to work with teachers, or how to make time for work and your children so that neither is neglected, or how to juggle relationships with friends while tending to your personal needs. The list goes on and on, and these types of things can be spelled out in a cheat sheet of tips that you can pass on to your mentees. It's just about telling them how we handled it. It doesn't mean you're telling them the way they *should* handle it, but at least it's providing them some ideas to consider when dealing with the issues women face.

If you're ready to find a mentor, I encourage you to follow any or all of these steps:

- Look for someone you have something in common with. I think it's really about starting with that connection.

- Consider the qualities you want to have and then find someone you can emulate. Who is someone you respect, and what is it that draws you to that person?

- Be your own mentor by living the traits you admire. Push yourself, develop your skills, learn what you need to know. As Cole writes, "The truth of the matter is that nobody worthwhile is going to mentor you until you start mentoring yourself."[11] Indeed. I have mentored many women, and I choose to work with those who have shown they are willing to do the work so I know my time won't be wasted.

- Take steps to build your confidence. Maybe you're at a place where you may not think you're good enough to seek the next level job in your career. This is a good place to start seeking advice from a mentor. Studies show that women mentors help boost women's confidence.[12] Mentees also feel like it gives them the type of encouragement and know-how when engaging with a woman who's supportive. I think it boosts their morale, as well. There's plenty of studies that illustrate those results.

- Attend women's support organizations. There are many female leaders or women in general who attend forums and events like The Women's Foundation, Women in Finance, Women in Law, and even organizations within your own company. You can meet women there who are very supportive of being a mentor because those are the kinds of women who attend these types of organizations and networking events. They're there to be supportive. I've met many young women who attended

---

[11] Cole, Nicolas, Three Ways to Attract the Mentor You Truly Want, The Ascent, https://theascent.pub/3-ways-to-attract-the-mentor-you-truly-want-fd5bd920347b

[12] KPMG Women's Leadership Study, Moving Women Forward Into Leadership Roles, https://home.kpmg/content/dam/kpmg/ph/pdf/ThoughtLeadershipPublications/KPMGWomensLeadershipStudy.pdf

an event where I was a guest speaker or panelist. Afterwards they'd ask me for my card, and then would email inviting me for coffee. It's a great way to meet women with like minds.

- Think in terms of specifics. What are the business skills you need to improve? You want a mentor who can give you the type of support and encouragement you need in the areas of development that are specific to you.

- Be teachable. A mentor cannot mentor everybody, so the mentor will also want to sign somebody they feel has the confidence to say when they don't know something and is, therefore, open to guidance. "If you aren't teachable, nobody is going to bother with you," writes Nicolas Cole. "And it has nothing to do with your intelligence, or your ability. It has everything to do with your attitude."[13] I have a lot of mentees, and they'll WhatsApp or occasionally email me and ask me questions out of the blue, saying "Oh I'm going through this. What do you think?" I love being able to help. Most of the time, I listen to their problems and tell them about similar experiences that I've gone through. As I mentioned, it is being able to give them a cheat sheet based on what I've been through or what I've seen others go through.

- Embrace curiosity. There is so much wisdom available from your female colleagues and seniors. "If you continue to do the same things and meet the same people, you will get stale pretty fast," writes Zalis. "Being curious, trying different experiences and connecting with all types of people is how you continuously evolve, stay relevant and be one of the most interesting people in the room."[14]

---

[13] Cole, Nicolas, Three Ways to Attract the Mentor You Truly Want, Ibid.

[14] *Zalis, Shelley, Why Mentorship Doesn't Have to be Formal,* March 2018 https://www.forbes.com/sites/shelleyzalis/2018/03/29/a-moment-of-mentorship-can-lead-to-a-lifetime-of-impact/#4b972e1579d2

- Be appreciative. Take time to reflect on the unique qualities and investment in your career that your mentor has given you. When I've seen my teachings manifest in one of my mentees, it gives me profound satisfaction. It makes me and any mentor want to do even more for other women when appreciation is shown for my efforts.

Remember, mentoring women can start at any time in their or your career. By being a mentor to an aspirational woman, you gain so much. In fact, you may find that you have just as much to learn from being a mentor. It reminds you of all the issues you experienced and what you overcame, and it reinforces the reasons why you wanted to support other women in the first place. Those issues are still out there. You gain satisfaction in seeing your mentee grow and helping to push the workplace forward for all women, present or future.

SPONSORSHIP: A GAME CHANGER

Remember what I stated at the beginning of this chapter: A mentor will talk with you, but a sponsor will talk *about* you. While mentors can have a significant positive impact on a woman's career, women also need an advocate—a sponsor—who is in the inner circle of leaders who make and influence talent decisions. A sponsor can speak up about you when job openings and talent discussions arise and throw your hat in the ring. Sylvia Ann Hewlett, CEO of The Center for Talent Innovation and author of *Forget a Mentor, Find a Sponsor: The New Way to Fast-Track Your Career* (Harvard Business Review Press, August, 2013), says that if you're going to win, you need a sponsor. "A mentor gives you friendly advice," says Hewlett. "A sponsor is senior in your organization or world and has the power to get you that next job. It's not about empathy."

Economist, founder, and CEO of the Center for Talent Innovation, Sylvia Ann Hewlett, explains: "Mentors can build your self-esteem and provide a sounding board – but they're not your ticket to the top."[15] Sponsors, on the other hand, can be that ticket. Sponsors take a direct role in the advancement of their protégés. Sponsors work at the same organizations as their protégés. They advocate for protégés, helping them earn raises and promotions and garner success in their shared environment. Sponsors put skin in the game, using their connections to advance their protégés through their endorsement and guidance. Having a sponsor, a career champion, is a game-changing asset that is especially important for minority and female professionals.

Jenna Goudrea agrees. In her article, "Why You Need A Sponsor— Not a Mentor—to Fast-Track Your Career," she discusses the "sponsor effect" as tracked since 2010 by the Center for Talent Innovation. "Four U.S.-based and global studies clearly show that sponsorship—not mentorship—is how power is transferred in the workplace. When it comes to getting ahead you need more than the counsel of a supporter; you need someone to advocate for you when you're not in the room. That takes someone who believes in you and has the juice to make it happen."[16] Millette Granville, Director of Diversity and Inclusion with Delhaize America described a sponsor as "an influential spokesperson for what you are capable of doing." Behind closed doors, a sponsor will argue your case. In the KPMG Women's Leadership Study, Dalynn J. Hoch, CFO, Zurich North America, says: "Having sponsors that put their own capital and credibility on the line for me helped me move into a number of leadership roles."[17]

---

[15] Hewlitt, Sylvia Ann, Sponsors vs. Mentors: What's the Difference & Why It Matters, Glassdoor.com, Jan. 2018, https://www.glassdoor.com/blog/sponsors-vs-mentors/

[16] Goudreau, Jenna, Why You Need a Sponsor—Not a Mentor—to Fast-Track Your Career, Business Insider, Sept. 2013, https://www.businessinsider.com/you-need-a-sponsor-to-fast-track-your-career-2013-9

[17] KPMG Women's Leadership Study, Ibid.

Attributes Of A Sponsor

The three main attributes of a sponsor are (i) they believe in your potential and are willing to take a chance on you; (ii) they are an influencer (i.e., they have a voice at the table), and (iii) they are willing to be your advocate, even without you asking for it.

As I mentioned, I've sponsored many women and men, but given that men usually have other male sponsors, I actively look for talented women. Most of the influential people in an organization are men and these men already spend a lot more time with other men. They go drinking with them, on business trips with them, lunch with them, etc. Naturally, a mentor/sponsor type relationship develops. Also, when companies sponsor an event for their clients, these events are usually sports events, such as ski trips, soccer games or Formula One race seats, and for the most part, it's men who attend such events.

Women may want to attend, but these events can take the entire day, and we may have other commitments, such as spending time with our kids. This results in these men having more direct access to clients and the senior male bosses and much more frequent bonding time with these bosses than the female employees. I've seen how men reap the benefits of this because as these senior men become even more senior, they bring these men up the ladder with them. The people who lose out are the women.

This is why when I spot a woman who is very talented, I make sure I find a way to help her get promoted or rise up. As one of the few senior women in an organization, if I don't do it, it is unlikely that anyone else would, either. I usually try to promote someone by mentioning her to other senior managers and saying that person is doing such a great job, and then talking to the business head, saying, "If there's a need for you to have someone who's very good in this role, I would recommend so and so."

Or if a business head would ask my views about someone and it is someone I believe in, I would be her advocate, basically pitching for her to get the role. In one situation, a business head asked whether this person really needed a title for a newly created senior role. I said, "Definitely!" She deserved to be recognized. Since he already had a COO in his department, I suggested CAO for her title. She got the role and the title.

Often an influencer will sponsor a person within the organization, and they didn't even ask for it since it usually happens behind closed doors. I've seen women doing a great job and knew they could and should be doing more. I'd ask them, "Are you willing to do more?" If the answer was yes, then when an opportunity arose within the company, I would recommend that person. I would then inform that woman about this opportunity and suggest that she go for it. You would think that they are all ecstatic about the opportunity, but there have been times when initially the women weren't sure if they could do it (i.e., they lacked the confidence) and were hesitant, but I would encourage them. Once they started the new role, they excelled at it because they are talented, smart, and very capable women.

HOW TO GET A SPONSOR

Attracting and keeping a great sponsor depends a lot on what you do. Unlike approaching someone to be your mentor and seeking advice, sponsorship must be earned. To do that, you must show a potential sponsor what you're working on, how you're doing on a presentation, how regularly you're participating in discussions during meetings, how often you speak your thoughts in terms of what can be done better, and more. If a potential sponsor sees that you are doing a great job, are committed to success, and care about the organization, they will eventually become a sponsor and speak highly of you in front of other people.

Pay attention to the leaders in your organization. See who has a track record of developing talent. Listen for leaders who praise their subordinates and have their backs when problems arise. These are the men and women you want on your side and to seek out for sponsorship or to at least make them aware of your contributions. Find them and then talk to them—the key is for them to get to know you so they will want to take a vested interest in your personal development and growth.

In a series of reports on sponsorship, Catalyst reported, "There is no 'silver bullet' for attracting the attention of a high-level sponsor."[18] While that is true, there are many things you can do to tip the odds in your favor.

Know And Make Known Your Career Goals

Where do you see yourself in one year, five years, ten years, or more? Are you clear on the steps you need to take to make it happen? If not, start there. Assess your skill set now, and determine the attributes necessary for the job you want to have. Once you're clear about your career goals, articulate them, as well as the skills you hold, the skills you're building, and the track record of execution you bring to the table. "This is the clincher," says Jo Miller. "If you are a demonstrated high performer and have clear career goals, sharing those goals with your manager, your mentors, and leaders can often be enough to enlist their sponsorship."[19]

Talk to your sponsor and mentor about your career goals and aspirations. Ask them for their views on how you can achieve those goals. By sharing your goals with them, they can help you get there or at least provide you with insight. If you speak to a sponsor and they

---

[18] Miller, Jo, The People Who can Open More Career Doors than You Ever Thought Possible, The Muse, https://www.themuse.com/advice/the-people-who-can-open-more-career-doors-than-you-ever-thought-possible

[19] Lean In, Women in the Workplace, Women are Doing Their Part; Now Companies Need to do Their Part, Too,

know what your goals are, when they hear of possible openings, they will recommend you for the position.

Also, if you don't have goals, seniors within the organization will think that you are fine in the position you are in currently. I remember during an annual review session when a woman was being considered for a promotion as Executive Director. There were several people there who said that this woman isn't ambitious and never even asked to be promoted to ED, and since there are such few spots, we should give that position to someone who really wants it.

MAKE YOURSELF VISIBLE

If you are someone who "stays under the radar" or "keeps your nose to the grindstone," that is great for getting the job done, but not for advancing your career. This was mentioned in the previous chapter, but it is worth repeating—you need to be visible. I keep seeing a lot of women who just put their heads down and think that's all they need to do is work, work, work, and do good, quality work. Yes, there are some managers who will see that and say, "Oh okay, great quality work. She should get promoted," but it only takes you so far. If influencers don't know who you are, your track record, or what you're capable of, they can't and won't support you.

"You can't expect a sponsor to put his or her reputation on the line when he or she doesn't know the quality of your work and what you're capable of," writes Jo Miller for themuse.com. "Your goal here is for the sponsor to see you in action and directly experience the quality of work you can deliver."[20]

So, raise your hand when you can. And start doing that now.

When I'm at a department meeting, I usually end by asking the group if anyone has any questions. I rarely get any questions. And if I do, it is usually from one of the guys. People are shy, embarrassed, or

---

[20] Ibid

worried that they will sound silly. But who cares? I always remember those people who do ask questions . . . not because they are silly questions, but because they asked. If they ask, they care. When I go to a conference or another speaker's event, I almost always ask a question. Most of the time, it is because I have a genuine question, but sometimes I do it because I want to be visible. People will remember those who asked. So, don't be afraid to share your ideas at meetings, make suggestions for improvements, ask to join a special task force, or be the speaker for a team presentation. The possibilities for increasing your visibility are endless.

Whatever you do, don't keep your accomplishments a secret! When you achieve something noteworthy, make it known to your leaders. For example, "If you bump into a potential sponsor in the cafeteria line, ask how he or she is doing," writes Miller. "Chances are he or she will ask you the same, so have a ready-to-share sound bite about a recent accomplishment, so you can respond, "I'm doing well. I just heard I've been nominated for engineer of the year!" Also, update your elevator speech and have it ready to go at all turning points in your career. You never know when the opportunity will arise for you to toot your own horn.

If you want to end up being a CEO or a COO or beyond, you must go above and beyond what you're doing and become more of a leader, become more visible, challenge ideas or systems that can be improved, and say things that show that you know the company and care about it. You must engage the company holistically. Do what it takes to be noticed and you will have a greater chance of getting a sponsor to choose you.

What About Men As Sponsors?

Mentorship and sponsorship must include men. In the wake of #MeToo, twice as many men say they feel uncomfortable mentoring women, according to research from *Lean In*. That's unfortunate because both men and women should grow together in order to advance equality in the workplace—we must be mentoring each other. We can learn a lot from men, and they can learn a lot from us.[21]

However, recent studies have shown men's increasing unwillingness to be an advocate for women. In a survey done by LeanIn.Org, it is clear that a growing number of senior men are afraid to mentor women. Results show that these executives are "worried about being accused of harassment, people thinking the wrong thing, or doing something that might make a woman uncomfortable."[22] Many men are worried that colleagues will say, "Oh, there must be something going on there," or "There must be some ulterior motive." One woman recently said to me she feels the #MeToo movement may have resulted in men acting very differently toward women; whereas, she said before they were joking around with her, and now they're hesitant to even joke around *near* her. They feel like they have to walk on eggshells and be careful. They're hesitant to sponsor women because they're concerned about putting themselves and their families in jeopardy.

I recently asked a senior male manager to sponsor a talented young woman. He said that he feels uncomfortable sponsoring her. He wanted a formal program from the company, such as a mentorship program, because he was worried about what other people may think if he suddenly spoke highly of her. He didn't want people to get the wrong idea. I told him that we can do this as part of the formal mentoring program, but he had to understand that we wanted him to be not only a mentor, but a real sponsor. He agreed to do so on this basis. I can understand why men would be worried. It used to be women who had to worry about their "reputation." Now it's men who have to actually worry about recrimination and false accusations. We need to find ways to reduce this fear in men because it is easy to see how these kinds of

---

[21] Ibid

[22] What Women are Up Against at Work, Survey Results, Lean In, https://leanin.org/sexual-harassment-backlash-survey-results

attitudes and behaviors will greatly impinge on communication and growth for all in the workplace. If we fall victim to tribalism in the workplace between the genders and the generations, gender parity cannot become a reality.

In a Facebook post, LeanIn.Org founder Sheryl Sandberg wrote that men's increasing unwillingness to mentor their female colleagues will have an adverse effect on opportunities for women at work. The Facebook COO pointed out that, "The last thing women need right now is even more isolation. Men vastly outnumber women as managers and senior leaders, so when they avoid, ice out, or exclude women, we pay the price."[23]

LeanIn.Org is launching a campaign called #MentorHer that urges men to use their power to support women in the workplace. We already know that mentorship and sponsorship are essential for career advancement and getting women to the top in leadership positions. "If we're going to change the power imbalance [. . .], we need to ensure women get more mentorship and sponsorship, not less," writes Sandberg. As mentioned before, many men are mentors or sponsors for other men because of their natural proclivity to find people who are like them.

If every senior person, male and female, sponsors a woman throughout their career within the organization, we will definitely have more female leaders. It's also incumbent upon the company to recognize that and challenge their leaders to find a female they think is talented and sponsor them.

WHAT COMPANIES CAN DO TO HELP

Companies can and should play a big role in the advancement of women in their organizations. Of course, we can talk about equal pay, flex hours, work-life balance initiatives, but in terms of what companies can do

---

[23] Sandberg, Sheryl, https://www.facebook.com/sheryl/posts/10159854933800177

in terms of developing more women in leadership through mentorship and sponsorship, they can do a great deal more. In the KPMG study,[24] working women said that companies that support women combined with women supporting women are the factors having the greatest capacity to drive growth in women's leadership. "In particular, many respondents believe it is critical for companies to most support a woman's career development during her twenties (80 percent) and career advancement during her thirties (61 percent)," the study found.

For mentoring and sponsoring to be successful, Liautaud argues that they need to be recognized as key to promoting the company's values, they need to be implemented across the workforce, and must be supported by founders and/or CEOs.

In companies, men need to get involved, too, she adds, not only to understand the aspirations and obstacles faced by high-potential women, but to act as mentors and recognize mentoring as a way of understanding the company in fast-changing environments.[25]

Talent Retention Programs

Talent retention programs, which should include at least 50 percent women, are very successful in keeping the best employees. Retaining women must be a key focus for all companies. It could start with a talent promotion program, making sure that there at least the same number of women as men, and then asking them to sponsor one of the women on the list.

These programs are successful when senior members (male and female) sponsor talented junior-level talent. That means they get to know them, assist them in becoming more visible to the

---

[24] KPMG Women's Leadership Study, Ibid

[25] Manciagli, Dana, How Mentors and Sponsors Help Women Succeed in Business, BizJournals.com, Oct. 2016, https://www.bizjournals.com/bizjournals/how-to/human-resources/2016/10/how-mentors-sponsors-help-women-succeed-business.html

organization, and let them know how they'll be promoting them within organizational needs.

The company can have a formal talent retention program, but as a part of talent succession planning or talent development planning, everyone in senior management should consider finding a female who is on this talent list to support and develop a relationship with. Some men, as I mentioned, don't feel comfortable sponsoring a woman, so it can help if the company has a formal program. But the point of the program must be to encourage senior managers to identify and find someone they're willing to sponsor, and keep looking out for someone who fits the bill.

Leadership Development Programs

Implementing leadership programs that develop and connect high-potential women with senior leaders is key to helping more women advance. A leadership program that is designed to make sponsorship easier for women to access—no matter what rung they are on the corporate ladder—benefits everyone. "Innovative corporate initiatives and senior female leaders can motivate and reinforce women on their way up the corporate ladder."[26] I believe when corporations make a commitment to moving more women forward, more women will shift from aspirational leadership to inspirational leadership much sooner in their careers.

I know that some large corporations will hire Executive Coaches for mid-level employees who the company would like to groom for senior management. I think it is an excellent idea, not only because it shows that the company is supportive of its staff, but these Executive Coaches can help these employees become better leaders.

---

[26] KPMG Women's Leadership Study, Ibid

When Hiring

When a senior position opens up, ensure that there are women who are interviewed for that position. If, for example, a company has a CFO position available, try to interview the same number of women as men. Sometimes headhunters may only refer men, but I think the company should insist that women should also be interviewed. Of course, the best candidate should end up getting the job, but at least we can be more conscious of interviewing a diverse pool of candidates.

A Mentorship Culture

Mentorship must evolve to include being part of a larger corporate culture in order to remain competitive and inclusive for all in the talent pool. According to Lois Zachary, Ph.D., author of *The Mentor's Guide*, building a mentoring culture is "the most important challenge" facing organizations today.[27]

Zachary describes a robust mentorship culture as one that is deliberate and focused on creating formal and informal mentoring opportunities throughout the organization. Mentoring programs can come and go, but a mentoring culture is sustainable. She explains that a "mentoring culture will be supported and valued within the organization. The programs within that culture create a standard and consistency of mentoring practice that really works."[28] By clearly setting expectations and consistently checking in, organizations set mentors and mentees up for success and increase the likelihood of a sustainable program.

When organizations establish the expectation that everybody is accountable for sharing support and knowledge, it builds a more

---

[27] Men as Allies: Engaging Men to Advance Women in the Workplace, Bentley University, 2017, bentley-cwb-men-as-allies-research-report-spring-2017.pdf

[28] Ibid page 69

qualified, committed, and happy workplace. In a business with a mentorship culture embedded in the mindset of individuals, "mentees (as well as protégés and others seeking professional assistance) benefit from wider access to opportunities which aid their professional and personal goals."[29]

It's been determined that many big mentorship efforts fail when they become too large to deliver the results they're designed to. In fact, big tech companies like PayPal prefer a constellation of focused mentorship programs, rather than one big company-wide melting pot of participants. For example, when there is a culture of mentorship, a graphic designer can mentor a budding artist in the mailroom, and a VP in Human Resources can mentor a marketing department junior. Successful mentoring programs have structure combined with informality combined with accountability.

"Just as an organization might have a plan to increase shareholder value, it's critical to have a plan for increasing sponsorship. Without commitment and a plan from the outset, sponsorship is not going to get to a point where it can be effective for sponsors, their sponsorees, and the organization," says Mike Fucci, chairman of the board, Deloitte. "Tools are not going to make it happen until you actually have a change in thought process where people think this is part of what they have to do to be a successful executive."[30]

Whether you are charged with setting up a program or you want to be the leader to initiate one, some important elements to consider include cohort size, educating participants about expectations and objectives, and defining time commitment. The CWB Bentley study emphasizes that programs must be tailored to the specific needs of the organization and employees, which means no two mentoring programs have to be the same.

---

[29] Ibid page 73

[30] Ibid page 79

Keep in mind, research shows that including men is essential. If men are not included, and not aware of the issues that women face with reaching the top, the more they tend to believe that gender diversity measures are unfair. When I tried to start a women's networking group within the company, there were men who just didn't see the need for it. They would tell me that women just chose to quit without realizing that perhaps the company could have done more to try to retain them. This is why building awareness among men is crucial.

In addition, I think if we label it as only for women and/or we don't have the buy in of all the senior managers (men included), it will be difficult for any such program to succeed. The better approach is to have talent succession programs, mentoring programs, and networking events for both men and women.

Cultivating a mentor or sponsor relationship is a journey of small steps and doesn't have to take hours upon hours of work. Identify what you want to accomplish, determine the skills you need to develop, and get to know the people who have exposure to the work you're doing. In the end, consider one action you can take today to strengthen your relationships and don't be afraid to ask. Your next mentor or sponsor could be sitting in the meeting or conference next to you ready and willing to help.

Chapter 8

Men as Allies

Men and women need to grow and evolve together by better understanding the issues impacting each gender in the workplace. We can learn a lot from men, and they can learn a lot from us. I think we are poised for a breakthrough in the workplace where gender (and generational) parity and partnership is a true possibility whose time has come, but we can't do it by ourselves. We need men as allies just as much as we need sisterhood. Increasing the numbers of women in leadership roles in every workplace requires that we engage men as supporters and drivers of change. Men and women have a joint responsibility to achieve gender equality. If most of the top positions are currently held by men, we can't make progress without their support and assistance in driving change. As stated in a speech by UN Goodwill Ambassador Emma Watson, the achievement of women's rights is a human rights issue and equality is everyone's business; we all have important roles to play in challenging cultural norms and stereotypes that limit us all and underpin violence against women and girls. We will not achieve equality without the engagement of men and boys.[1]

---

[1] Watson, Emma, Men as Change Agents for Gender Equality, Government Equalities Office, June, 2014, https://assets.publishing.service.gov.uk/government/uploads/system/uploads/attachment_data/file/396933/Report_on_Men_as_Agents_for_Change_in_Gender_Equality.pdf

Bringing men into the conversation on gender equality takes a step toward breaking down those expectations of both genders. As Watson said in her speech, "It is time that we all perceive gender on a spectrum, not as two opposing sets of ideals."[2]

With a growing number of men taking on the responsibility of caring for children as their partners work, breaking down traditional gender stereotypes is increasingly important. Research has also shown societal pressures to be aggressive and not revealing vulnerabilities can have negative effects on men. According to statics by the Center for Disease Control, suicide is four times higher among men than it is women. "Suicide needs to be addressed as health and gender inequality—an avoidable difference in health and length of life that . . . affects men more because of the way society expects them to behave,"[3] according to a report by Samaritans, a U.K.-based suicide-prevention organization.

Since equality is good for everyone, we should all want to achieve it. Business leaders should be fully aware that their businesses can only benefit by successfully attracting both men and women to their workforce. As mentioned in the previous Chapter, it is now an established fact that organizations with the most gender diversity outperform those with the least. Society based on respect for diversity and tolerance is good for women and men alike.

The campaign for gender equality has a long history, and each wave of feminism has seen men join the fight to improve the lives of

---

[2] Porter, Jane, Yes, Gender Equality is a Men's Issue, Fastcompany.com, Sept. 2014 https://www.fastcompany.com/3036289/yes-gender-equality-is-a-mens-issue

[3] Samaritans, National Suicide Prevention Strategies, https://www.samaritans.org/about-samaritans/research-policy/national-suicide-prevention-strategies/

women and girls. However, such men have been in the minority, and it is time for change.[4]

WHY IS THERE A LACK OF MEN'S ENGAGEMENT WITH GENDER EQUALITY?

Part of the problem, suggested Michael Kimmel, is that men don't see gender equality as being about them because—in the popular mind—gender, to them, means women. The "privilege of invisibility" means that those social groups with power are able to define themselves as the norm and see themselves as neutral, human, undefined by issues of gender, race, disability, sexuality, etc. For instance, many white people use the term "ethnic" to refer only to black and minority ethnic people, and the white identity is frequently underexplored and unacknowledged. Men's invisibility within the concept of gender is not an oversight but a privilege, and, Kimmel argued, privilege is invisible to those who own it. So one obstacle to men's engagement with gender equality is that men don't think it's about them.

Another is that while many, if not most, men agree with the concept of gender equality, fewer actively seek to divest themselves of privilege or make material sacrifices in order to create social change.

Finally, the gender equality area is traditionally dominated by women; therefore, it may be perceived as difficult for men to enter. This point is critical. We cannot afford to underemphasize how reluctant men are to enter feminized spaces – for reasons of fear of ridicule, fear of becoming "tainted" by femininity, and genuine concern that it is not appropriate for them to speak out about equality.[5]

---

[4] Men as Change Agents for Gender Equality: Report on Policy Seminar, June 2014, Government Equalities Office, https://assets.publishing.service.gov.uk/government/uploads/system/uploads/attachment_data/file/396933/Report_on_Men_as_Agents_for_Change_in_Gender_Equality.pdf

[5] Ibid, Men as Change Agents for Gender Equality, June 2014

Of course, not every man (or woman, for that matter) will support gender-equality initiatives. This tends to boil down to three common factors: apathy, fear, and ignorance. Apathy because some men are unconcerned about the issues or do not see why they should become actively involved. Fear because they are worried about disapproval from other men, losing status or privilege, or saying the wrong thing. And ignorance because they see gender equality as a "women's issue," they feel ill-informed about gender matters, or believe there isn't a problem. Helping men understand gender bias exists can make all the difference.

As Jackson Katz said in his TED Talk called "Violence Against Women - It's a Man's Issue": "A lot of men hear the term 'women's issues' and we tend to tune it out, and we think, 'I'm a guy; that's for the girls,' or 'that's for the women.' And a lot of men literally don't get beyond the first sentence as a result. It's almost like a chip in our brain is activated, and the neural pathways take our attention in a different direction when we hear the term 'women's issues.'"

This is also true, by the way, of the word "gender," because a lot of people hear the word "gender" and think it means "women." So they think that gender issues are synonymous with women's issues. There's some confusion about the term "gender." Once men begin to challenge traditional masculine norms and take a closer look at the negative impacts of inequality on men and women, they are more likely to back the cause for gender equality. When men experience gender norms as restrictive barriers in their own lives, there is a greater chance they will appreciate how these behaviours affect women.[6]

---

[6] The Role of Men in Gender Equality, Smart Group Corporation, http://www. smartgroup.com.au/sites/default/files/Upload%20documents/SMARTGROUP%20 The%20role%20of%20men%20in%20gender%20equality.pdf

RAISE AWARENESS

The reason we need awareness is that there are many men who don't realize there is even an issue. For example, Mike Gamson, Senior Vice President for LinkedIn Global Solutions, said, "I used to think that the world is fair. That it was a meritocracy. I no longer believe that. I think people who think it is an even playing field are probably like me—they have had it easy their whole life. They are probably a guy, they may be white, and they have likely been in the majority their whole life and they assume that it is like that for everyone else."[7]

"Several years back, halfway through our annual global sales kickoff, a woman on my team pulled me aside to ask if I had noticed that all the speakers on stage were male. I had a moment of realization – first of all, I hadn't noticed, and second of all, the reason for the gender imbalance on stage was that there were only men in charge of the respective departments. My leadership team was not a reflection of our broader team. It was a reflection of myself," he said.

It was an awakening that led to Gamson launching the LinkedIn Women's Initiative with the intent of supporting the advancement of women's careers. As a result, he increased the number of female senior leaders within the Global Solutions division from 6 percent to 30 percent in just a few years.

Several organizations, such as The Women's Foundation, have launched the Male Allies Initiative in an effort to leverage the "collective influence and personal engagement of male business leaders to advance greater gender equality together – within their organizations and more broadly across the Hong Kong business community."[8] Leaders from financial services, PR agencies, research institutions, manufacturing, law firms, and

---

[7] King, Michelle, Three Ways Men can Champion Gender Equality at Work, Forbes. com, September, 2017, https://forbes.com/sites/michelleking/2017/09/28/three-ways-men-can-champion-gender-equality-at-work/#58b80a823eb6

[8] https://mallieshk.org/

more agreed that women and organizations need male allies to help create a gender inclusive workplace. We need more initiatives of this type. The organization gives small cards to men to remind them of questions they should be asking themselves when they are at work.

For example, "Whose voices am I listening to and favoring in discussions? Am I making assumptions about this person based on their gender? Have I caught any biased attitudes and behaviors of my own? Do I refer to all colleagues in a comparable and respectful way, in and out of the office? How am I including company policies to achieve more inclusion and gender equality?" These are the types of questions that we should all be asking ourselves. Only then can we make ourselves more self-aware.

EDUCATE – GENDER PARITY BENEFITS EVERYONE IN THE WORKPLACE

Raising awareness also means explaining that gender parity benefits everyone in the workplace.

I've heard men say, "If that job goes to a woman, there will be less jobs for men," or "If she gets promoted, I won't get promoted." I find it surprising when men say this because it implies they would have gotten the job in the first place. If a company promotes based on merit, why would men be concerned? Don't we want the best person to make it to the top? If the companies we work for become more profitable because they have more women in senior management and its board, isn't that a win-win situation for all of us? Wouldn't we all want to work for a more successful and, according to several studies, a happier company? Don't we all benefit from that? I certainly would rather work for a successful company as a middle manager than an unsuccessful company as a senior manager. And if the company does well, it means there will be more jobs and more promotions, so in the end, we all win.

The truth is, the more diverse your company, the happier your company will be. In his book, *Angry White Men* ((Nation Books; revised edition, Apr 25, 2017) Michael Kimmel writes, "Equality, it turns out, is not a "loss" for men, in some zero-sum calculus; it is a win-win." Indeed, as women win, so too will men. "In our workplaces [. . .], we find that those companies that have implemented the best diversity training programs are also those where workers say they are happiest—and are therefore most productive, with the lowest turnover."[9] That includes men who also feel valued in those companies. When gender diversity and parity are done right, Kimmel concludes that "*everybody can get the opportunities and rewards they deserve*. Listening to the voices of *everyone* means just that."

Gerard Mestrallet, chairman of ENGIE, said, "Studies demonstrate that gender diversity and equality of opportunity can increase our overall performance as a company and we need to recruit a good mix of men and women." Making the workplace a fair and level playing field for women means better outcomes for men and women alike. Workplace gender equality is not only the just and right thing to do, it's linked to better economic performance. Workplace gender parity is associated with improved national productivity and economic growth, increased organisational performance, enhanced corporate ability to attract talent and retain employees, and a better organisational reputation.[10]

To enlist men as allies in the goal of gender diversity, it's essential to demonstrate what the benefits are *for men*. It is extremely important that men don't feel threatened or somehow grow frustrated by gender equality policies. These policies are not to treat the men less favorably than women. We must, therefore, ensure that gender policies are

---

[9] Kimmel, Michael, *Angry White Men: American Masculinity at the End of an Era*, Bold Type Books, April, 2017

[10] Ibid, The Role of Men in Gender Equality, SmartGroup

not perceived as exclusively benefiting women. We have to take this growing insecurity into consideration and adapt our communication and practices accordingly.

As much as women suffer from the effects of gender inequality, there are also serious problems for men. We cultivate more stereotypes about men than we think: we expect them to be strong, competitive, ambitious, sometimes insensitive. Masculine norms (for example, "be a winner," "don't show weakness," "be one of the boys") in a "command and control" management environment is often linked to stress, depression, and safety risks for men. Skewed representations of masculinity put men under pressure to show physical and emotional strength and to provide financially as the family "breadwinner." Men have a greater tendency not to recognize or respond to their own negative emotions, and this may result in more chronic and severe emotional responses to adverse life events. In addition, men who follow career paths in caring roles traditionally held by women can be subjected to discrimination.[11]

Research shows that men released from the pressure to be the provider enjoy relationships of greater equality, stability, quality, and intimacy. It's good for men's friendships with women, too. Gender parity also affords men the space and time to build closer relationships with their children, which much research shows benefits all individuals within families.[12]

All this illustrates just how gender inequality can be a challenge for both men and women, and how vitally they need each other to create change. While women are said to often hit a glass ceiling, men are pressured not to hit the glass floor. As leaders, as managers, our role is to reassure men and make them allies—if not advocates—of gender balance by showing them that diversity policies benefit all, women and men alike. (KPMG Women's Leadership Study).

---

[11] Ibid, The Role of Men in Gender Equality, SmartGroup

[12] KPMG Women's Leadership Study Ibid

Shobana Kamineni, executive vice chairperson, Apollo Hospital, says, "Maybe we should be arguing more in favor of 'gender balance across the organization,' instead of saying that we need to 'get more women to the top.' Inclusive environments allow more people to flourish irrespective of their personalities, communication styles, sexuality and other aspects of diversity. Collaboration and teamwork have proven links to productivity, creativity, innovation and enjoyment of work.

WHAT CAN MEN DO

Unfortunately, as I have mentioned, research from *Lean In* shows that "the number of men who are uncomfortable mentoring women has more than tripled since the recent media coverage on sexual harassment." In fact, they are "uncomfortable participating in a common work activity with a woman, such as mentoring, working alone, or socializing together.[13]

An article for SHRM.org by Kathy Gurchiek, titled One Year After #MeToo and 'Weinstein Effect': What's Changed?, discusses employee relations and the "Weinstein Effect." Gurchiek writes that there is an uncertainty of what constitutes sexual harassment that has made many men uncomfortable around female co-workers and "wary about how to navigate changing workplace dynamics."[14]

Johnny C. Taylor, Jr., SHRM-SCP, president and CEO of SHRM, states that there is a troubling trend where executives are "going as far as to not invite female colleagues on trips, to evening networking events or into their inner circles to avoid any situation that could be perceived incorrectly, thus reducing the opportunity for women."

---

[13] Men: Commit to Mentor Women, Lean In, https://leanin.org/mentor-her

[14] Gurchiek, Kathy, One Year After MeToo, What's Changed, SHRM, October, 2018, https://www.shrm.org/resourcesandtools/hr-topics/employee-relations/pages/sexual-harassment-workplace-weinstein-effect.aspx

Given that we already know women get less mentorship and sponsorship necessary for career growth for all the reasons illustrated in this book, this means things are getting worse and going in the wrong direction.

Adam Grant, Professor, Wharton School of the University of Pennsylvania, wrote in INC.com, "Thank you, Harvey Weinstein—and legions of other men who have abused their power. You haven't just hurt the victims of your assault and harassment. You've also done lasting damage by scaring decent guys away from creating opportunities for women."[15]

There are many things we can encourage men to do in order to help achieve gender parity in the workplace. Here are some suggestions:

1. Be accountable for parity.

As Adam Grant writes, "If you invite the dudes on your team out for a meal or on a work trip, do the same for the women. Also, team trips to strip clubs were gross in the 20th century. Surely that kind of misogynistic event has no place in workplaces of the 21st."

2. Run toward your discomfort instead of away from it.

Rather than a fight or flight response, Grant suggests men embrace the option called "tend-and-befriend." Women are more likely to tend-and-befriend; while men are more likely to fight or flee. The tend-and-befriend response focuses on the desire to build a nurturing relationship and seeking social support and attention. Seeking out social support and nurturing others is not only a great form of stress relief, it's also vital to our health. According to Shelly Taylor, a professor at UCLA who, along with her colleagues developed

---

[15] Grant, Adam, Men are More Afraid to Mentor Women in a Post-Weinstein World. Here are 3 Reasons to Do It Anyway, Inc.com, https://www.inc.com/linkedin/adam-grant/men-afraid-mentor-women-heres-what-we-can-do-adam-grant.html

the "tend-and-befriend" theory of stress response", although this "tend and befriend" theory of stress response is more common among women, there's no reason men can't show it toward women."[16] Interpersonal communication is key. Ask women directly what they are and are not comfortable with; share with women what *you* are comfortable and are not comfortable with.

3. Build mentor networks.

Try mentoring in small groups if one-on-one networking makes you wary. Grant reminds managers that it's more efficient for mentors because you don't have to repeat the same advice over and over again, and it might be better for mentees, too. "When I polled my students about preferences for office hours, they voted strongly in favor of group sessions rather than individual ones. They enjoy learning from the questions their classmates ask and comparing notes on the conversation afterward."[17]

4. Examine double standards and obstacles faced by high-potential women.

As one man said to me, "My female team member gave birth a few weeks ago and now she is back in the office. Because parental leave is only offered to women [as maternity leave], if women take it, it is assumed that they are not serious about work. This is all part of unconscious bias."

Awareness of these double standards can help. One way is by examining language with a gender flip. Ask yourself, *"Would I really have said that if I'd been talking to a man?"* That can be a real eye-opener. "Ask a man at least as often as you ask a woman to

---

[16] Taylor, Shelly E., Tend and Befriend, Sage Journals, Dec 2006, https://journals.sagepub.com/doi/abs/10.1111/j.1467-8721.2006.00451.x

[17] Ibid, Grant, Adam

do the office administration, work parties and other 'office chores' that are so often thought to be more suited to a 'female skill set.'"

5. Collaboration is the new key to success.

I think it's getting men to understand that we're not taking jobs *away* from them . . . it's about women representing 51 percent of the population and the fact there's fewer than 10 percent of women at the top. It's just making sure that there's fair representation through collaboration. They say women are the ones who make the decisions in terms of buying certain products. We are the largest consumer, so why wouldn't we be more representative in these companies? At the end of the day, we're all selling something, and we're the consumers. Collaboration works.

6. Be open to new ways of doing things.

Again, look at the studies. If you have diversity, people in the company will be happier. Women need a support system at work, which also improves things in the home. Women tend to drop out because they feel like, "Wow, I really can't handle all of this." A lot of it is being a little bit more flexible with the time. It could be men and women having more flextime and being able to work from home.

In "Violence Against Women—It's a Man's Issue," a TED Talk with Jackson Katz, he says, "One of the powerful roles that men can play in this work is that we can say some things that sometimes women can't say, or, better yet, we can be heard saying some things that women often can't be heard saying. Now, I appreciate that that's a problem, it's sexism, but it's the truth. So one of the things that I say to men, and my colleagues and I always say this, is that we need more men who have the courage and the strength to start standing up and saying some of this stuff, and standing with women and not against them and pretending that somehow this is a battle between the sexes and other kinds of nonsense. We live in the world together."[18]

Katz continues, "Well, the bystander approach is trying to give people tools to interrupt that process and to speak up and to create a peer culture climate where the abusive behavior will be seen as unacceptable, not just because it's illegal, but because it's wrong and unacceptable in the peer culture. And if we can get to the place where men who act out in sexist ways will lose status, young men and boys who act out in sexist and harassing ways towards girls and women (as well as towards other boys and men), will lose status as a result of it."

WHAT WOMEN CAN DO

Although research shows that men are less supportive than women of initiatives aimed at achieving gender equality, this isn't necessarily due to malice; instead, it's more likely to be caused by ignorance of existing inequalities. We can help increase the number of men as allies by doing certain things to increase awareness.

Here are some things we can do to do our part in creating gender parity in the workplace.

- Talk about it with men.

Making men aware of gender issues means women have to be willing to talk about it. Broach the subject with men in the workplace. Ask what they think about the ramifications for them about #MeToo. Ask them what makes them uncomfortable in the workplace. Tell them what makes you uncomfortable. You'd be

---

[18] Katz, Jackson, Violence Against Women—It's a Men's Issue, TED Talks, Nov. 2012, https://www.ted.com/talks/jackson_katz_violence_against_women_it_s_a_men_s_issue?language=en

amazed how much men are willing to share if we just give them the chance to do so and vice versa.

Ask the senior men to consider sponsoring a woman he thinks is talented. Explain to them that she does not have to be part of his team. Explain all the challenges women face in making it to the top, such as unconscious bias, and try to get them involved in effecting change. Even if you can get him to attend a seminar or panel discussion, can be the first step to awareness.

- Start in the home.

That's where opinions and attitudes are formed. I have two sons, and they know all the issues I go through. I talk to them a lot about it, so they're very aware. When they start working, I believe they'll be very supportive of women and gender parity. My husband is also engaged in these issues. He never knew it was so difficult until I would come home and explain the issues and challenges I have. He sees the double standards. He sees the increased expectations of women. He's more sensitive to it and in tune to it. He notices.

I've spoken to many men with teenage daughters, working mothers, and working wives, and I've noticed that the men who have working wives or daughters tend to be better champions of women, and have much more understanding of the issues we face. Those men are naturally more inclined and happier to engage. They see what their loved ones go through, so they're very supportive of women in the workplace.

I recently met a man at a panel discussion on the topic of gender diversity. He is a champion for women in the workplace, and when asked what made him become this passionate about it, he said that he was brought up by a single working mom, he has two older, very successful sisters, and his wife works in finance. He has heard about their issues and struggles, things that he has taken for granted. He realizes that the only way things can improve is if men get involved in helping to effect change. By telling our stories to the men in our lives, we can have more understanding and supportive men like him.

- Show that women support each other.

Remember to exemplify and personify sisterhood in the workplace. The behavior that we extend toward one another as individual women will reveal the kind of behavior that we can expect from men *and* women. We can't have one without the other. Do the PMS that I mentioned in the previous chapter—promote, mentor, and sponsor each other. If we do this, men will also start to promote, mentor, and sponsor women.

- Learn from men.

Men are better at raising their hands and asking questions. They're better at being visible. They're better at self-promotion and negotiating for better salaries, bonuses, and benefits. It's part of playing and winning the game . . . a man's natural instincts brought into the workplace. For example, men will apply for a job when they meet just 50 to 60 percent of the requirements, while women won't typically apply unless they meet 100 percent of the requirements, according to the *Harvard Business Review*.[19] I mentor junior women to just go for it and have the confidence that they'll grow into the job.

Some men like to have the final say, so that it appears as if it's their idea. I was on a conference call with about 20 people, and there was a guy who loved to take credit for everything. At the end of the call, I said, "Okay, we'll do these three things, and let's have

---

[19] Mohr, Tara Sophia, Why Women Don't Apply for Jobs Unless They're 100% Qualified, Harvard Business Review, August 2014, https://hbr.org/2014/08/why-women-dont-apply-for-jobs-unless-theyre-100-qualified

a conference call next week to follow up." Then he would say, "Yes, okay. Yeah, let's do these three things and have a call next week." I was thinking to myself, *There he goes again. He wants to be the one that has the final say so that people can remember him thinking that it was his idea.* I thought, *Okay, this time I'm not going to let him do that.*

Again, I said, "Yes, that's right. Like I said, we're going to do these three things, and let's have a call maybe Tuesday or Wednesday." Believe it or not, he did it again. He said, "Okay, yeah, these three things are great ideas, but why don't we aim for Wednesday." I thought *this is asinine.* But I also recognize that there are many men who want to have the last say because people remember it. That's a strategy. Finally, at the end I said, "Yes, Wednesday, three things. End of conversation. Goodbye," and I hung up.

- Take credit.

Men want to get credit. It's like getting "points" for them. I say, *Don't be a pushover.* Don't let men or women throw you under the bus. If it was your idea, find a way to make sure people *know* it was your idea.

My company had a big restructuring project, which required all departments to get involved, but I was proud of my team because we led the restructuring. Once it was completed, there was a meeting where the CEO thanked everyone, but especially pointed to a group led by another team. I was disappointed that we were not specially named given the amount of work that my team did, so afterwards I mentioned to the CEO that it was my team that led the project and he really should have highlighted that, instead of the other group. He said he knew that, but he wanted to give that other group some credit. I then suggested that he take my team who worked on the project for lunch to thank them. He ended up doing that, and my team was very appreciative of the gesture from the CEO.

WHAT COMPANIES CAN DO

It must be the tone that is set from the top. It's got to be the senior people—who currently are mostly men—recognizing that there are gender issues and making it a priority as a company to improve them. While it is imperative that individuals take action within the working day to build collaboration, it is also vital that companies demonstrate commitment to change through their actions and policies. Implementing top-down policies such as recruitment, promotions, sexual harassment, parental leave, and flexible working schedules to ensure gender parity are instrumental to success. Practices and programs like these need an entire book on HR practices to address them.

In addition, as clients, one of the first things that we can do is to expect gender diversity from the vendors we use. We can ask companies we use what they are doing to create gender diversity. Clients can be a catalyst for change. They can state that they only want to work with companies that have an adequate number of women in senior management positions and/or at least are doing things to make changes in support of diversity. I've asked the law firms that I use how many female partners are in their firm, the programs that they have to increase diversity in the firm, whether the client activities that they engage in are inclusive to both female and male partners, etc. It forces them to think about these issues.

Gender Awareness Workshops

I've asked our Human Resources Department to hold workshops that can bring issues about gender differences into the light. We must shed light on things that constitute sexual harassment or things that unfairly impede women's growth. Only by shining a light on these things can we not only create mutual understanding, but also nip inappropriate behavior in the bud.

Training can include identifying the differences in terms of unequal expectations of women and men. Let's talk about women's emotions. Let's talk about things like perceived or unconscious biases. Let's talk about the implication for #MeToo in the workplace. I once had a boss who just didn't know how to relate to women, and he was very uncomfortable talking to women. It was so obvious. He would just hang out with the guys. Oftentimes I thought, *Maybe he needs a training as to what the differences are and what the women's expectations are.* I think both his leadership and his relationships with his colleagues would have improved with more knowledge and understanding.

Companies can also provide immersion experiences, which offer men and women new roles so they can better understand how norms and assumptions create gender inequalities at work. These types of workshops and training engage women and men leaders in dialogue about what can be done to achieve gender equality. However, the key is making sure that people attend these workshops. Research tells us it's common for men in leadership roles to have negative attitudes to workplace education. Men in positions of power often expect they have little or nothing to gain from diversity and inclusion training. Management and human resources teams can shift pessimistic attitudes by building a compelling case for workplace equality through:

Companies should involve influential leaders. Participants are most likely to attend training sessions if they know their managers will also be there. Ask influential managers, especially men, to invite employees to participate in training and to assist in delivering content.

Reverse Mentoring

Reverse mentoring is when a subordinate mentors the senior person. Reverse mentoring is not a new concept. Jack Welch, while the chief executive of General Electric in the 1990s, required 500 of his top managers to pair up with junior workers to learn how to use the Internet.

It could be, for example, a young woman mentoring a senior man. Research shows men who have been mentored by women are more aware of gender inequality than men who have not had this experience. The gender power of reverse mentoring reveals issues that enable both parties to explore aspects of everyday life within the workplace. By pairing leaders with employees from different backgrounds, the senior mentee can become more empathic towards the challenges the mentor faces and help reduce unconscious biases. It provides a platform for solutions to progression problems and better outcomes. Not only that, the benefits tend to be two-way and multifaceted.

• Benefits

The senior level mentee learns what happens in their organization from a woman's point of view. He learns how that feels and the adverse consequences, and both will discuss what can be done to help. Cross-generational and other differences such as sexuality or ethnicity could also be explored. The mentor benefits from networking and being visible to senior management. Both mentor and mentee will offer his/her insights, and both will be learning from the other. The company benefits by having a more engaged and aware workplace that fosters mutual respect across genders, departments, and generations.

• Put into Practice

According to the Murray Edwards report, reverse mentoring works best most often when it is treated more like a conversation and less like a meeting with a packed agenda. Each conversation has its own rhythm and topic. "Some will want to work on implications and outcomes early in the process, and others will find it more comfortable to spend the first few sessions discussing issues and not outcomes." The mentor and mentee agree to check in with each other according to a schedule they set together. Conclusions and insights can be shared company-wide on an anonymous basis via monthly reports or through monthly meetings where individuals share the stage and share their findings.

- The Process

The company's role is to identify suitable pairing(s) based on objective criteria. Several members of a board or executive committee need to be mentees to facilitate learning from the perspective of women at different career stages. The guide to "Collaborating with Men" advises drawing up a reverse mentoring agreement that defines:

- Objectives – Overall purpose and discussion topics.

- What a successful outcome looks like – and any preparation and/or follow ups.

- Frequency of meetings (the guide suggests monthly or semi-monthly for one year and convened by the mentee) and agreement on the best form(s) of communication, which might not always be face-to-face.

- Guidelines for conducting this "workplace friendship" – this relationship works best if both parties share openly (what is not commercially sensitive information). This requires trust, tact, and patience. The company must make clear that there will be no negative career consequences for honesty, and personal information shared by mentees/mentors will not be shared without their consent and contribution. Also, there must be a process in place covering the circumstance if the pairing does not work or needs refining.

As Kevin Roose writes in his article for NYTimes.com, "Executive Mentors Wanted. Only Millennials Need Apply": "These programs are not just a departure from the business world's traditional top-down management style. They are also a sign of just how perplexed some executives are by the young people (and women) in their midst."[20] Junior office workers no longer want to be unseen and unheard and just toe the line, "many young professionals have a new mandate: Drag the boss into the 21st century."

In order for these programs to work, John Barrows writes in his article for HBR.org, "Why a Gen X CEO Hired a Millennial to Help Him Keep a Learning Mindset, that senior level men need to "Shelve the ego—and communicate." Barrows states that, "This whole idea of learning from younger employees, sometimes referred to as "reverse mentoring," can create tricky dynamics." After all, when you're the boss, "how can a junior colleague feel comfortable as the teacher, and how can I feel comfortable as the student?"[21]

Reverse mentoring requires having the confidence to be "humble about the knowledge or skills I need to gain." It also requires open and regular communication to keep the learning flowing freely in both directions.

Reverse mentoring can also include junior women and junior men to senior women. We have something to learn from everyone. Companies like Cisco Systems and MasterCard have experimented with these types of mentoring programs. "Inga Beale, 54, the chief executive of the insurance marketplace Lloyd's of London, has said

[20] Roose, Kevin, Executive Mentors Wanted. Only Millennials Need Apply, New York Times, October, 2017, https://www.nytimes.com/2017/10/15/technology/millennial-mentors-executives.html

[21] Barrows, John, Why a Gen X CEO Hired a Millennial to Help Him Keep a Learning Mindset, hbr.org, November, 2017, https://hbr.org/2017/11/why-a-gen-x-ceo-hired-a-millennial-to-help-him-keep-a-learning-mindset by John Barrows, Nov. 9, 2017

that her junior mentor, who is 19, has a 'totally different perspective' and leaves her 'inspired.' Melanie Whelan, 40, the chief executive of SoulCycle, holds monthly meetings with her younger mentor, whom she has credited with helping her get 'hip with what the kids are doing these days.'"[22] Of course, there are also benefits of young working mothers mentoring senior women about the challenges they face in the workplace that they themselves may not be aware of or, like mentioned in previous chapters, are hostile to the idea of "making things easier" for women when they didn't have it as good.

Evaluation of External Vendors and Events

You can tell a lot about a company by looking at where they spend their money and resources. A company that really cares about their employees has events that are inclusive and thoughtful. They ensure that diversity is something they are always thinking about. For example, companies should consider the following when examining consultants, speaking engagements, and vendors:

- Before sending employees to attend certain panels and conferences, ask about the gender balance of the event you have been invited to attend. Do the same, too, with events your leaders have been invited to speak at. Leaders can "make it a rule never to accept invitations where the panel will be all male."[23]

- If your company is asked to nominate a speaker at an event, nominate a woman to give the presentation. If your company is asked to pitch to a potential client, nominate a woman to lead the team presenting externally on behalf of your organization.

---

[22] Ibid, Roose, Kevin, Executive Mentors Wanted

[23] Ibid, Murray Edwards Collaborating with Men, https://www.murrayedwards. cam.ac.uk/sites/default/files/files/Report%202%20-%20Collaborating%20with%20 Men%20July%202017.pdf

- As mentioned earlier, when requesting bids from suppliers or consultants, ask about the gender balance of the team working on or pitching for your company's business. Just asking the question brings about awareness for other companies when they have to answer the question.

- Companies should ensure that client events or company-sponsored events are of interest to both men and women, or ideally, where the entire family can attend (such as charity walk-a-thon events). Some companies will sponsor events which result in mostly men attending (such as rugby games, all day golf events, or weekend ski trips). These activities are more conducive for men. Women may not want to spend an entire day away from the family.

These are very small steps that can make a very big difference.

Returnship Programs

When I decided to return to work at a law firm after being a full-time mom for four years, a senior partner at a large U.S. firm who interviewed me said he wouldn't hire someone like me because women with young children are not able to juggle family with work. So he suggested that I just stay at home and be a good housewife! I told him that whether or not I could juggle work with family was my decision to make, and not for him to make for me. As you can imagine, I didn't get the job.

Recently, a senior person in my team told me that he wasn't keen on hiring a particular woman because she took three years off work to be a housewife. He felt that this was too long of a period. I reminded him that I took four years off to raise my kids and that we should give this person a chance, as long as she meets all the other requirements. I told him that women who come back to work after being a housewife tend to be much better employees because they are self-motivated and diligent. We ended up giving her the job, and she turned out to be an excellent hire.

In an article for Telegraph.co.uk, Claire Cohen writes that in 2015, "an American study concluded what thousands of women already suspected: employers are more likely to hire an under-qualified candidate, than one who's taken a career break. It's no secret that women (and it is mostly women) who take time out of the workplace suffer discrimination."[24]

Indeed, an article for the *Telegraph* cites new research by PwC, Women Returners, and 30% Club[25], "two-thirds of female professionals end up working below their potential when they return to work after career breaks. Women returners (those who want to re-enter the workplace after a time out) are often faced with a triple whammy of bias: gender, age, and their perceived skills gap. They further found that 29,000 women returning to the workplace are forced to work fewer hours than they want due to a lack of flexible working."

According to the article, "They're seen as unambitious dinosaurs—having "chosen" to be mothers or carers, rather than scale the corporate pipeline."

Little wonder that, according to a 2014 study by the London Business School, 70 percent of women fear taking a career break. And those who do are often put off from attempting to return to the workplace at all. But things are slowly starting to change. Over the past two years, big business has woken up to the potential of "returners," and a number have launched formal schemes to help them dip their toes into the workplace again.

---

[24] Cohen, Claire, Why We Urgently Need to Solve the Return to Work Dilemma for Mothers, Telegraph.co.uk, Nov. 2016, https://www.telegraph.co.uk/women/work/why-we-urgently-need-to-solve-the-return-to-work-dilemma-for-mot/

[25] Telegraph Reporters, Thousands of working women forced into low paid, low skilled jobs after returning from career breaks, www.telegraph.co.uk, Nov. 2016, https://www.telegraph.co.uk/women/life/thousands-of-working-women-forced-into-low-paid-low-skilled-jobs/

Several companies have now launched career reentry programs to offer women and men an opportunity to try out the major transition back into the workforce. Workers who have taken years off from full-time work, either to raise children, help with elderly relatives, or deal with personal health issues, have been able to gradually return to successful careers by joining a "returnship program."

With respect to financial institutions, Goldman Sachs was one of the first to launch this program. Several large financial institutions, such as Goldman Sachs, now have a program for women who took leave from work for a few years to be a mother, and when they come back the company retools and retrains them. Goldman Sachs did it because they knew that these women can be incredible assets—they just need to be retooled and retrained.

The program, which is now copied by many other corporations, understands the value of diversity by helping to develop talented professionals who are looking to restart their careers after an extended absence from the workforce. The program was specifically designed for those who left the workforce for two or more years and are ready to return. It is a paid, eight-week program that offers opportunities in a variety of divisions and the chance to experience the vast network of resources at Goldman Sachs.

It is a wonderful idea since these returnships provide individuals with an opportunity to sharpen their skills in a work environment that may have changed significantly since their last experience as an employee. It also gives participants the ability to explore a new area of expertise and learn new skills; and at the same time, it helps banks find and (perhaps more importantly) retain talent that may otherwise have gone overlooked. The level of turnover among returnees is well below industry norms.

A more equal workplace would be a better workplace, and that would also help make a better world . . . for men and women, sons and daughters, and wives and husbands. By sharing best practice and research, peer-to-peer and junior-to-senior discussions, and concrete pledges to action, male and female allies who are versed in the subject of gender parity can help to drive real change in their spheres of influence. Normalizing and encouraging the conversation about gender and equality creates a safe workspace for all.

Men need to get involved and partner with women, not only to understand the aspirations and obstacles faced by women trying to advance their career, but to recognize the changes needed in order to understand and support a company's mission in a fast-changing environment.

Chapter 9

Confidence: The Ultimate Game Changer for Women's Careers

Women identify confidence as the key to leadership success. Throughout their professional careers, many women I have spoken with have told me they have struggled with their lack of it. Based on many different studies, it seems that girls and women struggle with it at various times in their lives. As moms, teachers, coaches, or surrogates, we all need to play a role in changing the way we raise girls so they become *more* confident as they become older. There are far too many examples of where the opposite is true.

When young women enter the workplace, studies show they are full of confidence, with 43 percent of female employees aspiring to top management roles, according to Julie Coffman and Bill Neuenfeldt in their research for Bain & Company, a management consulting firm. It speaks volumes that after only about two years on the job, "women's aspiration levels drop by more than 60 percent . . . with only 16 percent of women"[1] still thinking they can reach executive roles. What's worse, as women establish their careers, their confidence that they can achieve those goals drops by half.

---

[1] Standberry, Lindsey, Is This Why You're Not Getting Ahead at Work?, Refinery29. com, June 2015, https://www.refinery29.com/2015/06/89218/womens-confidence-gap-in-the-workplace

I have witnessed a lack of confidence in all levels of women's careers again and again—myself included. Far fewer women than men pursue promotions or ask for salary increases. When I ask women, "Why don't you ask for a promotion or a raise?" the reasons they say "I can't" are many. The most common are:

- they think they may not deserve it

- they're too shy to ask for it

- they don't know how to ask for it

- people will think they're too aggressive

- they don't want to be seen as difficult

- they doubt the quality of their work is good enough

- they are afraid that they may lose their jobs by asking for too much

- they are too nervous

- they're afraid the answer will be no

And that's what they say out loud! Imagine the things women say inside their own heads that exacerbate self-doubt and low self-esteem which, inevitably, sabotages their careers.

The Institute of Leadership and Management, in the United Kingdom, conducted a study in 2011, simply asking British women how confident they felt in their professions. Half of the women reported feelings of self-doubt about their performance and careers, while less than a third of male respondents reported self-doubt.

Linda Babcock, a professor of economics at Carnegie Mellon University and the author of *Women Don't Ask,* uncovered a similar lack of confidence among American women, with concrete consequences. She found, in studies with business school students, that men initiate salary negotiations four times as often as women, and that when women do negotiate, they ask for 30 percent less than men do. I've seen this many times. Women don't realize that if we don't ask, we won't receive.

Victoria Brescoll, Yale's School of Management, says, "There's just a natural sort of feeling among women that they will not get a prestigious job, so why bother trying." And when she asked about men's feelings? "Men go into everything just assuming that they're awesome and thinking, 'Who wouldn't want me?'" Brescoll says. In *The Confidence Code,* the authors say Brescoll is right. "Most of the men we interviewed, in addition to our colleagues and friends, say they simply spend less time thinking about the possible consequences of failure."

WHY IS CONFIDENCE LACKING IN WOMEN?

According to the women's leadership study by KPMG, a woman's view of herself as a leader begins to take shape early in childhood with the values she learns, her exposure to female leadership skills, and whether she has role models. Indeed, "Childhood lessons and early exposure to leadership have a significant impact on a woman's perceptions of her ability to lead. Professional working women surveyed saw themselves as 'smart' growing up and cited school and academics as the area where they most felt like a leader." Take a look at what women said about what they're taught: 86 percent say they're taught to be nice, only 44 percent recall being taught to be a good leader, and a dismal 34 percent say they were taught to share their point of view. Another 76 percent of respondents said they wish they had learned more about leadership when growing up.[2]

So, it starts when we're young. Young girls are taught to be compliant. It's actually easier for young girls than young boys to behave well, because our brains pick up on emotional cues from an earlier age. As girls growing up, we know where approval from teachers comes

---

[2] KPMG Women's Leadership Study, Ibid

from. We see that well-behaved girls who sit down and do their thing without being difficult receive kudos and attention from teachers. That's when the need for external validation of our behavior escalates. As a result, we learn that we are most valuable and most in favor when we do things the right way: "neatly and quietly."

In *Nice Girls Don't Get the Corner Office,* Lois Frankel, PhD, writes, "From early childhood, girls are taught that their well-being and ultimate success are contingent upon acting in certain stereotypical ways, such as being polite, soft-spoken, compliant, and relationship-oriented." But as Kay and Shipman write in *The Confidence Code,* "Confidence that is dependent on other people's praise is a lot more vulnerable than confidence built from our own achievements."

The result is that "making mistakes, and taking risks, behavior critical for confidence building, is also behavior that girls try to avoid, to their detriment. Research shows that when a boy fails, he takes it in stride, believing it's due to a lack of effort. When a girl makes a similar mistake, she sees herself as sloppy, and comes to believe that it reflects a lack of skill."[3]

According to Joyce Benenson, men repeatedly and universally score higher than women when measured for self-esteem. Even seven-year-old boys have more self-confidence than seven-year-old girls. "Men appear to be born believing that they are of high ability, whereas women do not easily assimilate to the idea that they are as good as others. Hundreds of studies show this effect and suggest that men just feel better about themselves than women do."[4]

"When a man, imagining his future career, looks in the mirror, he sees a senator staring back. A woman would never be so presumptuous," write the authors of *The Confidence Code.* "Underqualified and underprepared men don't think twice about leaning in. Overqualified

---

[3] *The Confidence Code,* Ibid page 88

[4] *Warriors and Worriers,* Ibid page 75

and over-prepared, too many women still hold back. On all levels, our talents are not being fully realized. We believe we're stalling because, all too often, women don't see, can't even envision what's possible."

It is a true and troubling phenomenon in our society that men are almost always more confident than women, even when the women are equally or more talented. Most women aren't comfortable dominating conversations, throwing their weight around in a conference room, interrupting others, or touting their achievements. Some of us have tried these tactics over the years, only to find that it just isn't our style.

The implications of this confidence gap are grave. We know that because women are more likely to be perfectionists and therefore avoid risks, they are less likely to speak up in meetings, ask for raises, seek promotions, and negotiate better salaries. Indeed, research shows there is a direct correlation that higher levels of confidence lead people to be more successful in life and in work. Kay and Shipman found that success correlates more closely with confidence than it does with competence. "Yes, there is evidence that confidence is *more important* than ability when it comes to getting ahead. This came as particularly unsettling news to us, having spent our own lives striving toward competence."

Ideal Woman

In her many books and workshops for men and women about men and women, Alison Armstrong has named this "disease to please" that is inherently female: The Ideal Woman. She is the ideal image in our head of what the perfect woman would do *in every situation*. Her job is to make sure you survive, and her belief is that you will only survive by being perfect.

She is in our head questioning our decisions, scaring us about things that may or may not even happen, and reminding us of the consequences of being wrong. "Her standard is perfection, and she'll settle for nothing less," says Armstrong. "The ideal woman has no concern for your happiness." If perfection is your standard, of course, you will never be fully confident because the bar is always impossibly high, and as a result, you will constantly feel inadequate.

Armstrong further explains that a part of being female and feminine is that we adapt. Women become whatever we perceive as valued. "The areas where you think you can still achieve something is exactly where the ideal woman keeps after you." Given the many reasons for not pursuing career growth listed at the start of this chapter, you can see The Ideal Woman takes a lot of women out of the game. The fear of making a mistake or not pleasing the ones in charge is rampant.

In *See Jane Lead*, (Business Plus, 2007) Lois P. Frankel, PhD writes that women who suffer from this "disease to please" make the risks associated with being in leadership much more daunting for women than they are for men. "They want everyone to like them. They think they need to do everything perfectly. They're inclined to do things by themselves rather than delegate. They don't want to disappoint anyone."

As Frankel writes it, this sounds very much like being a new mother. New mothers want to make sure their babies thrive and love them back. "They think that if they're not perfect, there will be some catastrophic result," writes Frankel. "Not wanting to look like they aren't good mothers, they are reluctant to ask for help." The additional responsibilities that come with motherhood are just on top of a woman's previous responsibilities, and women fear they will drop a ball (or their baby) and screw up something else.

"Eventually they learn there is no such thing as the *perfect mother*," Frankel writes. "Women need to apply this to their roles outside the home and understand there is also no such thing as the *perfect leader*."

According to Katty Kay and Claire Shipman, authors of *The Confidence Code: The Science and Art of Self-assurance—what women should know* (Harper Business, April 2018), "women feel confident only when we are perfect. Or practically perfect." Remember, women won't even apply for a job unless they can check all the boxes. With that as our collective and yet internalized personal standard, what room is there for confidence?

Perfectionism also keeps us from taking action. "We don't answer questions until we are totally sure of the answer, we don't submit a report until we've line edited it ad nauseam, and we don't sign up for that triathlon unless we know that we are faster and fitter than required. We watch our male colleagues lean in, whiles we hold back until we believe we're perfectly ready and perfectly qualified."[5]

Ruminating

A close relative of The Ideal Woman is a woman's ability to spin her wheels in negative thinking. In *The Confidence Code,* the authors write that women "spend far too much time undermining themselves with tortured cycles of useless self-recrimination. Simply put, a woman's brain is not her friend when it comes to confidence."

Studies done by Susan Nolen-Hoeksema, a psychologist at Yale, show that women have an instinct to dwell on problems rather than solutions, so they "spin and spin on why they did a certain thing, how well or (more often) how poorly they did it, and what everyone else was thinking about it." A woman's intensive capacity for brooding puts women at risk of anxiety and depression, according to Nolen-Hoeksema.

Mike Thibault, an NBA scout and former assistant coach for the L.A. Lakers, has spent ten years coaching women. Thibault says the propensity to dwell on failure and mistakes and an inability to shut out the outside world are the biggest psychological impediments for his female players, and they directly affect performance and confidence on the court. "There's probably a distinction between being tough on themselves and too judgmental," he said. "The best male players I've coached, whether it's (Michael) Jordan or people like that, they are

---

[5] *The Confidence Code,* Ibid page 106

tough on themselves. They push themselves. But they also have an ability to get restarted more quickly. They don't let setbacks linger as long." But women do.

An example of this is one of my girlfriends who started her own business. She did it for several years, but the business failed. As a result of this failure, she never wanted to start another business. She had excellent ideas for a new start up, but when I suggested that she try again, she said she was too afraid. She was paralyzed about starting another business because she was afraid to fail again.

David Rodrigues, Vice President of Human Resources at Marriott, says that if things go wrong, he just shrugs them off, saying "I don't dwell on stuff; when it's done, it's done." Kay and Shipman said they heard the same attitude from most of the men they interviewed. "Even when they aren't natural performers, they just move through their challenges with less baggage."

IMPOSTOR SYNDROME

According to Dr. Sandi Mann, senior psychology lecturer at the University of Central Lancashire, Director of the Mind Training Clinic, and author of *Ten Minutes to Happiness* (Robinson, 2018) writes, "impostor Syndrome is a condition affecting more and more successful women where sufferers of the condition view their work success as luck rather than ability."[6] Impostor Syndrome refers to individuals who are highly successful but unable to internalize their success. They experience intense feelings that their achievements are undeserved. Many women feel they're terrible frauds who aren't cut out for the job and live in fear of being found out.

---

[6] Mann, Sandi, Why Do So Many Successful Women Suffer from impostor Syndrome?, Daily Mail, Sept. 2018, https://www.dailymail.co.uk/health/article-6222071/Why-successful-women-suffer-impostor-syndrome.html

In *The Confidence Code,* the authors write that before Facebook COO Sheryl Sandberg published her book *Lean In,* she said, "There are still days I wake up feeling like a fraud, not sure I should be where I am." I think a lot of us at times feel the same way— i.e., how could we possibly deserve to be so successful. When I was promoted, I thought to myself that I'm very lucky that my bosses supported me, rather than attributing it to my talents or qualifications.

Jess Cook is a chief executive officer of public relations and says, "I first realized I suffered from impostor syndrome in my mid-20s when I was picked from a pool of 1,600 candidates for a graduate position with the advertising giant M&C Saatchi. I was terrified I'd be told they'd hired the wrong person. My psyche insisted the achievement wasn't mine." Like so many other outwardly successful women, Cook says, "Whatever I do, I never feel it's good enough and then I relentlessly brood over what I didn't make happen rather than on what I did."[7]

Dr. Mann further writes that impostor syndrome isn't just a case of low self-esteem. "It's a distinct pattern of thoughts and behavior that are alarmingly common, especially among women," writes Mann. "It makes sufferers believe they're a terrible fraud, whose best is never good enough, and whose lack of capability for their highly lauded roles will soon be 'discovered.'"

A review article published in the *International Journal of Behavioral Science,* titled *"The Impostor Phenomenon",* found that an estimated 70 percent of people, the overwhelming majority female, experience these impostor feelings at some point in their lives.[8]

It becomes a self-fulfilling prophecy where the more a woman accomplishes, the worse the worry about being "revealed" becomes.

---

[7] *The Confidence Code,* Ibid

[8] Sakulku & Alexander, "The Impostor Phenomenon," International Journal of Behavioral Science, 2011, Vol. 6, No.1, https://www.tci-thaijo.org/index.php/IJBS/article/view/521/pdf

"In the process it batters self-esteem, drains self-confidence, impacts on mental well-being, and affects personal relationships," Mann states.

In *The Confidence Code,* the authors found that women, from lawmakers to CEOs, expressed an inexplicable feeling that they didn't own their right to lead. "Too many of the fantastically capable women we met and spoke with seemed to lack a certain boldness, a firm faith in their abilities." They discovered that, for many powerful women, just discussing the subject is uncomfortable, for fear of revealing some embarrassing weakness. "If *they* are feeling all that, only imagine what it's like for the rest of us."

Success is equated with external factors

Women tend to equate their value based on things such as praise, appearance, or just plain luck. In *Lean In,* Sandberg writes that when a man is asked about an accomplishment, he will typically equate his success with his own innate qualities and skills. On the other and, if you ask a woman the same question, "and she will attribute her success to external factors, insisting she did well because she 'worked really hard,' or 'got lucky,' or 'had help from others.'" Sandberg further found that men and women differ in their explanations for failure: "When a man fails, he points to factors like 'didn't study enough' or 'not interested in the subject matter.' When a woman fails, she is more likely to believe it is due to an inherent lack of ability."

According to Joyce Benenson, from early in life, girls and women don't take credit for what they have achieved. "Girls and women are much more likely than boys and men to attribute their successes to luck. Blaming luck diverts attention from a woman's own competitive efforts and avoids potential retaliation."[9]

Further, our obsession with physical appearance adds to our need for external validation and drains our confidence even more. "Even the

---

[9] *Warriors and Worriers,* Ibid page 176

most accomplished, beautiful, and celebrated human beings you know don't get a nonstop stream of compliments and positive feedback."

Oftentimes, there is no feedback at all, leaving women second-guessing themselves and wondering what they did wrong, thinking that they didn't look good enough, or questioning if they'll do anything at all the next time due to self-doubt. "When our confidence is based on external measures, the biggest risk is that we won't act. We are more likely to avoid risk if we think we might feel a dip in approval," writes Kay and Shipman in *The Confidence Code.* "Chasing permanent praise can lead to self-sabotage."

Fear (Whether Of Taking Action, Failing, Or Not Deserving)

Women are so obsessed about getting everything exactly right that we fail to take action because we're terrified of doing something wrong. But, without taking risks, women will never reach the next level. As Sheryl Sandberg writes, "Women need to shift from thinking 'I'm not ready to do that' to thinking, 'I want to do that—and I'll learn by doing it.'"

According to *The Confidence Code*, women will tell themselves there's no point in trying because their past failures prove they aren't good enough. Whereas men will shrug that failure off as an inevitable consequence of external forces which have nothing to do with their ability. The result is that their confidence remains intact.[10]

Dr. Frankel says that another reason we continue to hold ourselves back is that "we can't see beyond the boundaries that traditionally circumscribed the parameters of our influence." In fact, women have learned that it's dangerous to go out-of-bounds. As Kay and Shipman write in *The Confidence Code*, "In the most basic terms, what we need to do is start acting and risking and failing and stop mumbling and

---

[10] *The Confidence Code*, Ibid page 106

apologizing and prevaricating. It isn't that women don't have the ability to succeed; it's that we don't seem to believe we *can* succeed, and that stops us from even trying."

At Manchester Business School in England, Professor Marilyn Davidson asks her students what they expect to earn, and what they deserve to earn, five years after graduation. "I've been doing this for about seven years," she said, "and every year there are massive differences between the male and female responses. The male students *expect* to earn significantly more than the women, and when you look at what the students think they *deserve* to earn, again the differences are huge."

I have heard female colleague after colleague expressing some version that they don't "deserve" the right to own their own success or the right to ask for a raise. Some have said, "Oh, maybe my department's not doing well enough right now," or "I don't feel like I deserve it. I haven't really added much value this year." Well, if you think you don't deserve it, you don't deserve it. But if you have worked really hard, and you think you *do* deserve it, it's time to ask for what you deserve instead of worrying that you'll be seen as demanding or difficult or out-of-bounds.

I remember thinking about whether or not to ask for a raise. I was afraid to ask because I was worried that the response would be a "No." I was rationalizing that maybe they will think I'm being too pushy or difficult, so I probably shouldn't ask. Then my husband said, "You are the one that goes around saying to people that you shouldn't be ashamed to ask." And I thought, "Oh, but you know, maybe because it's really not the right time to ask." He said, "You work your butt off. You should be asking for a raise." Sometimes it's just that nudge, that reinforcement, that *hey, why aren't you doing that*, and not feeling guilty about it. Ultimately I did ask, and I ended up getting a well-deserved raise.

So, don't be afraid to ask and don't fear the answer in advance. What if they do say no, right? It doesn't mean that you're not qualified. It just means that, in that particular year, it's not going to happen. That doesn't equate to the quality of your work. If you think you deserve it, you should ask. As Lynne Doughtie, U.S. Chairman and CEO-elect of KPMG, says, "Own your career. Don't wait for someone to tap you on the shoulder and present an opportunity to you."

As the president of Nasdaq, Adena Friedman says, "Just say yes. Use any fear as motivation to be successful. That fear will then turn into confidence." In other words, run toward your fear—in turn, it will build your confidence.

HOW CAN WOMEN BUILD CONFIDENCE?

The good news is, it's possible to dramatically increase your confidence. And the easiest way is to get out of your head and take action. Here are some suggestions for boosting your own confidence in the workplace and beyond.

Eliminate Your Inner Demons

Alison Armstrong says, "The only way to take Ideal Woman out is to *expose* her—subject her to public ridicule." This means talking to your trusted friends and colleagues about what is going on inside your head and what Ideal Woman is saying to you about your standards for perfection. It is amazing the amount of laughter and relief women feel when they expose that mean, nasty, judgmental woman talking incessantly inside their heads.

The authors of *The Confidence Code* recall that they both spent too much time in their twenties and thirties being stuck in self-doubt and internalizing setbacks.

But how many of us would do the same thing, focusing on the negative feedback, instead of the positive? When I give my reviews to my subordinates, I always start with the positive and maybe have one or two areas of improvement. I find that it is usually women who have an issue with the areas of improvement. Rather than appreciating all the positive feedback, they are focused on that one area of improvement, and they are disappointed. We all need to remember that the only way we can get better is to know what these areas of improvement are, and work on them. Be proud of the positive and be grateful that someone is actually telling you how you can be better at what you do, because most people don't get that kind of valuable feedback.

As Dr. Mann writes about the impostor syndrome, the first thing she tells her clients is to acknowledge the problem and recognize it for what it is. "When that voice in your head murmurs that they'll 'find you out,' you can square up to it. As soon as you name it, you control it." Dr. Mann recommends that you start by writing down the *facts* . . . such as, you graduated with honors, you aced a project, you were promoted because of x, y, z, etc. "Is it realistic to feel (like an impostor) given the evidence to the contrary?"

When presenting or part of a panel discussion, if few women were present, I used to doubt whether I was good enough to be part of the group. I would feel deflated and asked myself repeatedly whether I deserved to be there. My inner voice would say that I'm an impostor and that I'm not good enough to be here. Now, I've learned to stop my inner voice by telling myself, "Yes, I do deserve it. Yes, I am good enough!"

And remember, the fact that you're constantly striving to improve (albeit through self-doubt) is a good quality. You can also acknowledge you don't have to be perfect to be successful. "Once you have grasped that self-knowledge, you'll realize the only impostors in your life were the sham feelings cheating you out of the success that is truly yours," writes Mann.

Take Action

As Kay and Shipman write in *The Confidence Code,* "Confidence is about action. It also takes repeated attempts, calculated risk taking, and changes to the way you think." Women may resist taking action because we are afraid of failure, but failure is an inevitable result of risk taking, and it's essential for building resilience. We've often heard motivational speakers say that the secret to success may be, in fact, failure. By failing, we learn from that experience to be better equipped to deal with issues later.

"Nothing builds confidence like taking action, especially when the action involves risk and failure," the authors write. "Risk keeps you on life's edge. It keeps you growing, improving, and gaining confidence. It's okay to start simple."

Confidence is a choice . . . whether to act, to do, or to decide on a course of action. "If you choose not to act, you have little chance of success. What's more, when you choose to act, you're able to succeed more frequently than you think."

They further state that if you only remember one thing from their book, let it be this: *When in doubt, act.*

Toot Your Own Horn

Women should not feel apologetic or shy about flagging their successes. Men do it all the time. The authors of *The Confidence Code* found that, "A man is usually comfortable going to his boss with a big smile, a high five, and a loud boast about his awesome triumph." You can do the same. Encourage your friends, colleagues, and mentors or mentees the importance of taking credit for their accomplishments and the importance of letting their employers know. It's possible to do so without sounding like a braggart. For example: "Did you hear we won the new account for branding services? I'm so proud of my team."

Speak Up

Even though it is hard, women need to speak up. I have seen women in board meetings who have really great questions, simply because they look at things differently than men in a way that is so positive for the company. I understand why research shows that having women on the board really helps organization—both in morale *and* the bottom line. If women are on the board, a company is less likely to engage in misconduct, for example.

But again, the women who get on boards are those who are confident enough to speak up. However, I find that a lot of times when I enter a conference room for a meeting and there are women there, they're not very vocal. They sit behind everyone else in the room, rather than at the table. Or even if they sit at the table, they don't really speak up, even if they have a good question.

As outlined in *The Confidence Code,* "We know that most women tend to talk less when we're outnumbered. We go into a meeting, study the layout, and choose to sit at the back of the room. We often keep our thoughts, which we decide can't be all that impressive, to ourselves. Then we get cross with ourselves when the male colleague next to us sounds smart saying the same thing that we would have said." I know this to be true, because it's definitely happened to me.

Don't Take it Personally

When you face a problem at work, remind yourself that it is about work and it isn't about you. If your boss tells you that the document wasn't well drafted, resist the temptation to see it as a personal attack. We have this habit of thinking too much and dwelling on our mistakes. Thinking about things again and again won't solve the problem. As mentioned, men find it much easier than women to shrug off any negative comments.

As studies have shown, while many women seek out praise and run from criticism, men usually seem unfazed and are able to discount other people's views much earlier in life. "From kindergarten on, boys tease each other, call each other slobs, and point out each other's limitations. Psychologists believe that playground mentality encourages them later, as men, to let other people's tough remarks slide off their backs."[11]

According to Jamie Friedlander in her article for www.success. com, "Many women fall behind where they could be excelling. While

---

[11] *The Confidence Code,* Ibid Page 91

they second-guess the tone of their boss's offhand comment or dwell on whether they should suggest a bold idea in a meeting, their male counterparts brush off potentially negative comments, confidently speak up and eventually pass them by."[12]

I have seen male bosses brush off criticism and attacks very easily. Once my boss's boss called for him, and since he wasn't around, I took the call. That boss told me to tell him that if he continues to never be around to answer his call, he can forget about having a job. I was shocked and worried for my boss. I nervously told my boss what his boss said, and he just brushed it off and said, "If he wants to fire me for meeting with clients, then go ahead, I can easily get another job." I was so impressed that he could brush it off like that. If it were me, I would have panicked and been really worried about it.

In the book, *The Male Factor: The Unwritten Rules, Misperceptions, and Secrete Beliefs of Men in the Workplace,* (Crown Business, 2009) Shaunti Feldhahn cites that women's inability to move on or to take things personally is one of the top pet peeves men have about women. "Men are simply not wired to take things as personally as do women," she says. "To them, work is just business; it's not personal. If women want to be seen as having the stamina to play in the big leagues, then they need to take personal out of the equation."

The message seems to be loud and clear: *Get over it.*

Grow Your Knowledge Base

Confidence requires a growth mindset because *believing* that skills can be learned leads to *doing* new things. It encourages risk, and it supports resilience when we fail. That way, confidence is less about external validation and more about what you make of yourself.

---

[12] Friedlander, Jamie, Why Women Struggle With Confidence More Than Men, Success.com, Feb. 2017, https://www.success.com/why-women-struggle-with-confidence-more-than-men/

Many studies show that great leaders are the people who are constantly improving, learning, and doing more . . . both personally and professionally. I've often told my mentees that "knowledge is power", so increase your knowledge base. One way to do this is by reading or listening to books. I love Audible books, because whether I'm walking somewhere or waiting in line, I will listen to something . . . anything that helps me improve. I've listened to books about leadership, business management, mentorship, and even *confidence.* Paying attention to these things means I'm always trying to self-improve.

The more you grow your knowledge base, the more you grow your confidence. If you want to be the CEO of a company, you can't just do it knowing one area of development. If you show that you really add value to the company and really understand the company and are educating yourself and evolving, those things add to your credibility, which then adds to your confidence. When employers see that you're knowledgeable, they will come to you and ask you questions. If you can answer them, it builds your confidence.

One woman told me that she wanted to take a course about how to be a director in a company. She said, "Oh, but the company won't pay for it, and I don't know if I have the time." I said, "If you can afford it and this is something that's important to you, make the time and do it. Sign up for it and pay for it because it will add value to yourself." If it's about personal development, you have to make the time and investment. Make time to network, attend meetup groups, join industry seminars and conferences, and learn everything you can.

Change Your Thoughts from "You" to "Us"

OSU psychologist Jenny Crocker has found that women thrive on *we.* She found that when young female graduates stop thinking about how they can prove themselves and instead think about how they can improve things for their colleagues or their company, they get a big boost of automatic confidence. The attention is no longer on themselves and what's going on in their heads. *The Confidence Code* shares how Crocker has used that research to create a helpful tip for public speaking: "Reframe your remarks in your head. Tell yourself you are speaking on behalf of the team, or the organization, or for the benefit of others, rather than for yourself. It's a simple, practical way of moving that spotlight off yourself and onto others to give you confidence."

Take Up More Space

"The use of space is one way we make a statement about our confidence and sense of entitlement," writes Frankel in *Nice Girls Don't Get the Corner Office.* "The more space you take up, the more confident you appear." Frankel advises women to notice the differences between how men and women sit on an airplane or on the subway. "Whereas men sit down and spread out using both armrests, women tend to keep their elbows tucked in close to their sides, trying not to take up too much space."

Sitting up straight, taking up more space, and making eye contact can all help give you a short-term confidence boost.

Recognize and Emphasize What's Inherently Yours

LQ and EQ refer to "likability quotient" and "emotional quotient." In *See Jane Lead,* the authors write, "Although IQ certainly contributes to success, LQ and EQ factor more prominently into the behaviors of effective leaders." Your IQ is something you're born with, but your LQ and EQ determine how far it will take you—and they can be developed.

This is where women have the edge. Research conducted by Dr. Jean Greaves, Dr. Travis Bradberry, and Lac D. Su of TalentSmart, a global consulting firm specializing in developing human capital, indicates that when it comes to EQ, women score higher than men in overall measures of emotional intelligence, and in three of the four emotional skills: Self-management, social awareness, and relationship management. Those are skills that are inherent to women and ripe for effective leadership.

ENSURE WOMEN ARE HEARD—SENSITIVE WAYS TO AMPLIFY POINTS MADE BY WOMEN IN MEETINGS

The Murray Edwards College, University of Cambridge report on *Collaborating with men: From research to day-to-day practice* offers a wealth of information about "sensitive interventions" and "making meetings better" that can enhance workplace experiences for women and men . . . and, therefore, the company.[13]

It is true that men tend to dominate conversations in mixed groups, and women who experience this find it demoralizing. Rather than being a bystander, men and women—when made aware of the problem—can intervene in a sensitive way to stop this from happening. People are, or can be, understandably reticent to intervene during a meeting in a way that exposes them to criticism. Colleagues need suggestions on how to intervene effectively.

For example, during a meeting, if you see that a woman's idea has been ignored or misappropriated, say something like, "Yes and, as Kelly said . . ." or "That builds on a point raised by Kelly earlier," and repeat the point. In addition, chairs/meeting conveners need to consciously intervene when women are interrupted, and invite them to finish their point.

For Elaine Chao, the secretary of transportation whose family moved to the U.S. from Taiwan when she was a child, says confidence

---

[13] Collaborating with Men 2017, Murray Edwards College, University of Cambridge, https://www.murrayedwards.cam.ac.uk/sites/default/files/files/Report%202%20-%20Collaborating%20with%20Men%20July%202017.pdf

in the workplace means ". . . encouraging people, particularly women, to push themselves, to take on tasks that they think are beyond their reach, like leadership." While it's true that pursuing a top position seems daunting, remaining at the same level does nothing to increase confidence. The authors of *The Confidence Code* say, "The trick is to recognize that the next level up might be hard, that you might be nervous, but not to let those nerves stop you from acting."

When asked what advice they would give to future generations of women, more than two-thirds of respondents in the Women's Leadership Study indicated confidence—being confident in their capabilities (75 percent) and confidence to ask for what they deserve (67 percent)—is the key advice they would pass along. Women in the Sisterhood can start right now. "Every leadership position is a stretch," Chao says. "No one ever thinks they're born a leader, that this or that leadership position is perfect for them. It is always a stretch. We should just encourage young women to stretch more."[14]

With brave effort and support along the way, we can all choose to expand our confidence. But we will get there only if we stop trying to be perfect and start being prepared to fail.

Support Your Sisters and Be a Role Model

By now, this goes without saying, but it bears repeating anyway.

Always look for opportunities to build up the reputation of your female colleagues. Compliment them in meetings. Provide constructive feedback in private. Recommend women for promotions. And by all means, "disengage from conversations where women are gossiping about other women." In *Nice Girls Don't Get the Corner Office,* Frankel writes, "You can simply walk away, or you can show even more courage by saying you think you all should be supporting, not ragging on, women in the office."

---

[14] KPMG Women's Leadership Study, Ibid, page 21

We can also help each other by giving each other permission to act. Like I've said, one little nudge is all I've needed on many occasions where my confidence may have been lacking. "Rather than repeatedly telling your friend she's great, try encouraging her to take action instead," write Kay and Shipman. "Often, it takes just one suggestion—one comment from a friend or coworker—such as, 'You should consider that city council seat' or 'I'm sure you could handle the supervisory job.'"

Or simply just, *Go for it.*

Conclusion

According to the U.S. Census and Department of Labor, women make up 51 percent of the population of the United States. Although it is a slim margin, there are more women than men to fill roles in the workforce. Yet, the majority of senior management positions are held by males. In the U.S., slightly more than one-third of senior managers were female. Globally, that number is significantly lower—24 percent.

Why the gap? Is it because women are not capable? Not qualified? Not interested in climbing up the proverbial ladder and hitting that glass ceiling? My experience and research show that the gap has nothing to do with talent, qualifications, or capabilities. I also know that there are many women who want and deserve to hold management positions. In my opinion, women are in a jeopardized position—they are competing with men, and they are simultaneously competing with each other.

Yes, as if there aren't enough obstacles to overcome, such as parenting, home and family, stereotypes, and the mentality that executives are defined as men in suits, women have historically held themselves back from their own success. By refusing to stand up, speak out, express their desires, and make themselves recognized, they tend to become wallflowers in the promotional candidate pool.

If that wasn't challenging enough, women are active participants in the sabotage of their careers. Every time we put another woman down, we drag down all of our sisters. Every time we equate a woman's appearance with her skills and talents, we judge a book by its cover . . . without attempting to read a single word. In doing so, we support the notion that women should be seen and not heard and that a woman's value is based solely on her appearance.

This is true of women who are low on the workplace totem pole, as well as those who hold mid or upper management positions. By not supporting one another, voicing our capabilities and strengths, we voluntarily become active participants in holding each other back.

This isn't just my opinion. This book is abundant with studies and research that reveal the stark disparities between men and women in upper level management positions, each providing a plethora of supporting reasons why it is so. I believe it is because women act alone—they were taught to look after and support men and our family, but nobody taught us the necessity of looking after and supporting each other. We are more than half of the population, but we are not unified.

The concept of sisterhood addresses the issues we face in the workforce, why they are present, and how we, as a group of unified women, can create a path up the corporate ladder that will benefit not only us as individuals, but women as a whole.

Sisterhood is defined as female siblings—I'd like to take that one step further and state that it is a group of female siblings in the labor force. Just like within a family unit, in a work unit, women all face the same obstacles. They've been victims of the same stereotypes and have the same unique challenges. As mothers, daughters, sisters, and friends, we wear many hats that can impede our climb up the ladder.

What can we do about it? We can push each other up! We can help each other get up that ladder, one rung at a time, until we are no longer the minority, but at least equal members of the management club. Only when female executives are the norm and no longer the exception will we be recognized as powerful candidates in the promotional pool. One woman at a time, we can build each other up, rather than knocking each other down, so that as a group, we can all enjoy the benefits of career success and advancement.

The best way to inflict change has been the subject of argument for decades. As sisters, I believe the best way to change the makeup of the executive and supervisory population is to use one of our greatest strengths—the power of influence—to shift the mindset that keeps us in positions of low responsibility (and low pay) to one where the sky is the limit.

"Play like a girl" is a sports saying that has turned a negative into a positive, allowing people to see females as competitive athletes in a male-dominated sports world. Let's adopt that thinking as we boost each other up in a male-dominated C-suite world.

Let's stop the sibling rivalry and have our sisters' backs. Let's erase the inferiority complex we've painted ourselves with for years. Let's treat ourselves and each other as we'd like to be treated. Let's be sisters through thick and thin, and stand united as a force that cannot be ignored.

I invite you to join me on this mission. Use the information in this book to create awareness and then become an active proponent of my message. Reach out to other women and seek advice, offer assistance or praise, recommend them and give them credit for their ideas and contributions. Seek a mentor, then become one. Sponsor a deserving woman who can benefit from your knowledge and experience. Give her a hand up, and network with women from multiple levels and industries, sharing stories, ideas, and most of all, solutions.

We are worthy. We are deserving. We are one. United, we create a sisterhood that has tremendous power to change the trajectory of our careers and lives.

Charles Malik once said, "The fastest way to change society is to mobilize the women of the world." I wholeheartedly agree. However, I know that women are reluctant to speak up and speak out and gain well-deserved recognition. The fear of rejection and criticism holds them back and keeps them at status quo, where they suffer in silence.

It's no secret that we've been told that men have more power than women. Unfortunately, we accepted that as fact and sealed our fate.

I propose, though, that we recognize our unique power. We don't have to wait for a title and corner office to have power. As sisters, we don't have to wait for someone to give us our power. We already have it.

Sisters, it is time for us to use it.